NORMATIVE BEHAVIOR

Andrew Oldenquist

UNIVERSITY
PRESS OF
AMERICA

For Nina and Mark

Table of Contents

PREFACE AND ACKNOWLEDGMENTS

This began, in the late seventies, as an impatient polemic against recent ethical treatises, and then gradually got tamed until it became another one. It seemed to me then, and still does, that philosophers had an interest in proving the rationality of ethics that was manic and unhealthy, as though their ultimate nightmare was putting their best, airtight, moral argument on the board and having a class of sophomores drawl, "Well, I guess you and I have different values systems." No physicist has to risk that kind of humiliation and the philosophers strove to fashion deadly refutations that would give them similar security. At the same time the effects of the mindless relativism of the sixties and seventies were becoming apparent, especially as preached to school children and practiced by criminal justice professionals. Both the relativist and moral intellectualist alternatives seemed wrong and distasteful.

During the mid 1970's there began a rekindling of interest by a number of thinkers in human nature, evolutionary history, and the idea of Man as part of nature, as these bear on the nature of ethics. I suspect this direction of late twentieth century thought is still gathering momentum. The "new naturalism" is not definist but descriptive, seeking to understand its corner of the universe, which implies, of course, that causes are not merely to be distinguished from moral reasons and set aside but integrated with reasons and explored as part of the process of naturalizing ethics. In any case this is what I try to do. The theory that will emerge is relativistic at a deep level: deep enough, I believe, to provide no solace to either criminals or education professors.

It was natural, then, that I should see the work of Charles Stevenson as a starting point and it is to him that I owe my first acknowledgment, for rewarding discussions and extensive written comments on draft chapters, made by Stevenson about a year before his death. I am indebted to a number of collegues and ex-collegues--to Mary Williams for introducing me to issues of evolution and human nature, to the late Wallace Anderson for numerous probing and sensitive criticisms, to Boris Nikolaichev and Ruben Aprecian for tough-minded critiques of my idea of letting loyalties compete with ideals; and to my wife Riek for moral support and for tolerating a lot of dithering. I am particularly grateful to William Lycan for reading nearly every word of my early draft and disagreeing usefully with much of it; and to Alfred Mackay for numerous genial and penetrating arguments about the issues of the book. Kenneth Long made most of an index and Erdinc Sayan was an admirable, over-qualified proofreader. The philosophy departments of The Ohio State University, Moscow University, and Oberlin College provided me with forums for public discussion and criticism.

The Ohio State University College of Humanities provided much appreciated financial assistance in the preparation and publication of the book, and the University's Mershon Center provided me with generous support during the writing of my examina-tion of loyalties and patriotism. I wish to thank the editors of the following journals for permission to include passages from articles I wrote: MIND, "Rules and Consequences," April 1966; THE JOURNAL OF PHILOSOPHY, "Universalizability and the Advantages of Nondescriptivism," February 1968, and "Loyal-ties," April 1982; THE PERSONALIST, "Evolution and Ethics," January 1978; THE AMERICAN PHILOSOPHICAL QUARTERLY "The Possibility of Selfishness," January, 1980.

I. ETHICAL THEORY AND LOST INNOCENCE

1.1 <u>Introduction.</u> A virtue descriptive ethics shares with geology and sanitary engineering is that its problems, however difficult, are ones we are sure are solvable. Would that we could say the same about normative ethics. We <u>know</u> that people act in ways that are called right and wrong, they utter moral sentences, make righteous speeches, argue, praise and blame one another, deliberate, feel guilty, and appeal to principle. These are phenomena, data, and they are what, collectively, I call normative behavior. When we confine philosophical ethics to the investigation of normative behavior there is no question but that there is a subject to investigate and a truth to be found, just as there is regarding any other corner of the universe about which empirical facts are organized and theories proposed. Someone may prefer to substitute "best theory" for "truth"; either way, there are no grounds for greater diffidence about descriptive ethics than about geology or paleontology.

There is a philosophical and a taxonomic reason for calling this study "normative behavior." First, I do not mean behavior that can or should be judged normatively, but rather the kinds of behavior, and more, an anthropologist must explain to understand his tribe's values and morality. However, the title also indicates an element of the theory that will be developed. I shall be arguing that moral beliefs are kinds of aversive or supportive dispositions from which it will follow that if someone believes that A is immoral he is disposed to act against A. One way to do this is to attack A, another is to sincerely say, "A is immoral": each of these is a bit of normative behavior. Moral judgment will turn out to be (generic) moral action—a kind of normative behavior and hence itself subject to moral appraisal; a consequence will be that a few more pieces of the puzzle of morality will fall into unsurprising positions.

1

This is not a book about normative ethics but an attempt to develop a plausible theory that explains the phenomena. Yet, without any question there will be implications for normative ethics, particularly in the chapters on universalizing and reasoning. Most books on ethics, including those in the twentieth century "analytic" tradition, attempt to produce knock-down, iron-clad proofs of substantive moral principles. To this end modern moral philosophy has deluged us with one "logical" or "conceptual" gimmick after another: definitions of "rationality" and the "function of ethics," rule utilitarianism, constitutive rules, neo-Aristotelian functional accounts of normative words, various neo-Kantian arguments, and game theoretic deductions from rational self-interest. These books get refuted or picked to pieces in the philosophical journals almost before the ink is dry on their pages.

My own view about normative ethics can be put quite simply: Humans are innately social animals who must indoctrinate their young in rules that permit us to live together in a way that is reasonably safe, satisfying, and predictable. These rules are our social morality and on a basic level are the same or nearly the same within every tribe and culture on the face of the globe: Honesty, fairness, incest prohibition, pair bonding, and keeping unwanted hands off other people's bodies and property. But I cannot prove that we should be social or even survive. I cannot deduce "oughts" from "is's," juggle smart selfishness until, when it lands, it turns into morality, nor can I invent a logical funnel into which we pour conflicting principles and at the bottom collect their resolutions.

More recently, philosophers have taken up casuistry; this is to be applauded, though not because students find it relevant: for them casuistry often is an excuse for avoiding difficult or abstract thought. An ancient function of moral philosophy is neither normative nor casuistical but is the attempt to understand a corner of the world. The corner with which this book is concerned contains the phenomena I call normative behavior.

By contrast with much recent writing in ethics, there is something very pure about the work of

Charles Stevenson, who wished to understand those social, linguistic, and psychological phenomena we call morality. The theory I shall defend shares more than its general purpose with Stevenson's work. His basic insight, which is that moral beliefs are aversive or supportive dispositions and moral utterances manifestations of these dispositions, is capable, I believe, of being developed in such a way that the standard objections that were made to ETHICS AND LANGUAGE are no longer serious.[1] This is one of the things I attempt, although the theory that emerges differs in a number of ways from the emotive theory and its prescriptivist offspring, and it considers a number of issues the emotivists ignored. I shall be at pains to show that the theory I defend permits rational moral argument, or at least, permits it as well as does any other theory.

It is commonly believed that moral philosophy is not like science because there has not been any dramatic increase in the body of relevant evidence since Thales. Indeed, it is thought that we should not speak of evidence but of a given set of data, like the Bible, which the philosopher hopes to explain with a new felicitousness. A paleontological theory might elegantly explain the present osteological evidence, and a new bone turn up tomorrow that refutes the theory. But in ethical theory, it is said, there aren't any new bones, just new ways to relate old ones, these new ways being the distinctions and "conceptual points" with which ethical treatises are replete. My theory, like others, contains some rearrangement of the familiar. But I raise some metaphysical questions about the self and some causal questions about the basis of what people value and think worthwhile, and for the latter, biological, anthropological, and psychological evidence is relevant.

Twentieth century moral philosophers doted on the meanings of words and sentences. One reason for this was the ascendency of the analytic-synthetic distinction, which gave them hope of discovering, if only they analysed hard enough, analytic truths with which to refute sceptics, relativists, and immoralists. When analytic truths went out of fashion, they pursued the same goal with "conceptual points." The focus on words resulted in insufficient attention to moral beliefs, these being nonlinguistic items which someone not acquainted with recent tradition would naturally think would be a primary target of investigation. In the account of the nature of morality presented here moral belief is the pivotal notion. Since I argue that moral beliefs are dispositions to be for or against something and not truths in any exciting sense of "truth," the theory can be called non-descriptivist, or better, emotivist. I do not systematically set out to refute the doctrine that there exist moral properties or uniquely moral facts. The test of the theory, as with any, is how well it accomplishes the positive task of explaining the phenomena.

A compelling argument against the view that there exist moral facts in addition to ordinary physical facts is Gilbert Harman's argument in the first chapter of THE NATURE OF MORALITY.[2] Harman argues that moral facts are not needed to help explain moral observations in the way in which physical facts are needed to help explain physical observations. Thus, the fact that people have certain beliefs about physical theory and electrons will not explain a track on a cloud chamber; we have to suppose, in addition to our having certain beliefs, that an electron actually went by. However, in order to explain a person's clear sense that a particular act of cruelty was wrong it is enough to appeal to the fact that he has certain attitudes and beliefs about cruelty; we need not suppose, in addition to his having certain beliefs and attitudes, that there was a moral fact present in the situation. One could argue, I suppose, that moral beliefs and attitudes require moral facts to explain them. For the full exposition of the argument I refer the reader to Harman. In what follows I assume a similar conclusion, and here and there hazard arguments, but I hope to persuade more by the virtues of a competing theory than by an elegant refutation.

A theory's survival depends on how much it explains and on the number and seriousness of the intellectual embarrassments it is forced to incorporate. A good ethical theory ought to provide clear and plausible answers to the following questions:

(1) What do "right" and "wrong," etc., mean, and what is a moral belief?

(2) How is ethics rational?

(3) How do reasons for and causes of moral beliefs relate to one another, and what, at the deepest level, are these reasons and causes?

(4) What is the extent and significance of the universalizability of moral judgments?

(5) How does self-interest relate to morality and how does morality relate to society?

These are some of the main questions I try to answer; they are very general and ought to be taken up in any systematic philosophical book about ethics. In addition there are questions it particularly behooves a theory of my kind to answer:

(1) How are moral dispositions (attitudes, approvals) different from nonmoral ones?

(2) If moral sentences do not state facts, how can they be the premises or conclusion of valid arguments?

(3) What do moral words mean?

(4) More generally, if there are no moral facts, no eternal moral truths, why should we take morality seriously and why shouldn't we see Hitler's morality as no worse, "objectively speaking," than any other?

The point of the first question is that an adequate theory should be able to tell moral approvals and aversions from ordinary loves and hates, likes and dislikes. The solution will be to devise a purely descriptive list of features, which I call the marks of the moral, such that when enough of them apply to an approval or aversion we can be reasonably sure that we have a case of moral belief rather than a case of mere liking or aversion.

5

There are also questions that the theory I propose can answer and which other theories ignore or cannot answer very well:

(1) Why are we inclined to morally criticize people for their moral judgments rather than treat such judgments as mere mistakes?

(2) Can we identify moral beliefs and judgments independently of the use of any peculiarly moral vocabulary?

(3) How can we account for the different degrees of strength or intensity with which two people might hold the same principle, and which produce moral disagreements that do not depend on disagreement about either facts, logic, or principles?

(4) How can we understand the notion of loyalty or "community," which seems to share features with both egoism and morality and to set limits on our willingness to universalize?

(5) How can someone's moral belief have evolved, genetic causes, and at the same time be something he believes because of his reasons?

If the theory I propose can cope with the second set of questions and give good answers to the third, it will well accord with the moral phenomena, with current science, and with a conception of Man as an innately social animal whose values and behavior are the joint product of environmental and genetic causes. The theory that results is naturalistic in the nineteenth century sense of the term. What is offered is not proof and the neat tying up of all loose ends and problems, which is quite beyond my power, but rather a sufficient assault on the problems to give a ring of truth to the kind of theory it is and to the direction in which it aims. Readers with very pure ideas of what philosophy should be may think that some of the hypotheses that follow belong to the social sciences and that others, particularly in Chapter Six, belong to biology. However, I do not find such distinctions to be very clear and I have ceased to care about the boundaries of academic turf;

in any case, a philosopher should propound what he thinks is plausible, within the limits of his training and habits of inquiry, without regard to where what he says is thought to "belong."

1.2 Are We Sunk Without Moral Facts? I have been told that moral monsters will like my early chapters. If so, they are also bad philosophers, with a false idea of what the basis of morality must be if we are to take it seriously. The lost innocence Kant said led to scepticism and relativism could be cured, he thought, only by a metaphysics of morals that grounded moral truth. I wish to show that what ruins one's sense of the seriousness of morality is the loss of a sense of moral community, not the loss of truth or the rejection of moral facts. Moral facts, whatever they might be, are of no importance. The disease that causes amoralism, as well as much immorality, concerns love and alienation, not lost truths. Here I wish to introduce the problem and in Chapter Four begin the development of an answer.

By an amoralist I mean someone who believes that anything he does is all right if he really wants to do it. Few people are perfect amoralists and most sometimes feel a worm of doubt at the back of their brains: a suspicion that they might be doing bad and selfish things and rationalizing about it. The imperfect amoralist resents these doubts and is indignant at the suggestion that his worm of doubt is "the moral law within." It obviously makes a difference, he tells himself, whether his doubts represent fossil emotions from his childhood or intuitions of moral truths that are seeping through his rationalizations. He may conclude that if moral beliefs are attitudes, he can adopt the "fossil emotion" interpretation of his doubts and qualms; they are now merely inconvenient feelings in need of exorcism. Borrowing Nietzsche's language, our amoralist wishes to be the monster filled with joy and not the pale criminal, and getting rid of moral facts, he may believe, allows him to have his wish. However, if the amoralist is concerned at all that he might be doing bad and selfish things he already is the pale criminal, regardless whether or not he thinks there are moral facts and moral truths.

7

A truly amoral person is not just someone who rejects certain theories about the nature of morality, he is someone who simply does not care about the reasons people have for judging things right and wrong. Someone for whom nothing is right or wrong might know how to wield moral words, know what principles are generally accepted, and know how to discern the nature and consequences of an action as well as the next person. Indeed, in telling us "what would be right and wrong were there any such thing" he might be more perspicacious than most people and be accepted as a reliable moral expert. What then would he lack? He would pass a written test in normative ethics with flying colors. David Hume or Francis Hutcheson might say that he possessed everything requisite for morality except the moral sense, by which they would mean the capacity or disposition to affectively respond to what he discerns. This is on the right track. An amoralist does not care what happens unless it affects himself or people and things dear to him. He does not care if strangers or people who are not his friends are hurt, robbed, deceived, or treated unfairly and, as he puts it, he simply does not <u>want</u> these things to happen to himself or to his friends. The person who truly does not care what happens to others either has not been socialized or has suffered mishap such as great trauma or genetic defect; in any case we cannot refute him and, more importantly, very probably cannot reach him.

A more common, related condition is ethical relativism. One or another form of relativism may be thought to be a consequence of the theory I defend. For if there are no moral facts and you and I disagree in a way that cannot be settled by logic or the nonmoral facts, must we not concede that you have your opinion and I have mine and that neither is more correct or "any better" than the other? In the absence of either moral facts or the commands of an unquestioningly accepted divine authority, must we not concede that what is "right for you" may be "wrong for me," these expressions serving to communicate the view that there is no ground or basis on which the act is right <u>simpliciter</u>? One might attempt to defend what I will call the unanimity thesis, which is the view that if people agreed about logic and the facts they would agree about morality.

8

But if a basic moral belief is just an attitude, and attitudes fall short of being real morality, what difference does it make how popular it is? If it is a mere attitude, does it not remain so even if everyone shares it? At least, this seems to be what we must say if what we require to make morality more than a matter of "mere attitudes" is the existence of moral facts and not just societal authority or agreement. In Chapter Five the unanimity thesis will be examined in detail.

When someone says that what is wrong for him or her may be right for someone else, he may be led to think that morality is a slight matter if anything at all. Consequently it is important to determine how we should view morality as a whole if we reject certain traditional grounds of moral objectivity, including religious grounds. In the eighteenth century Richard Price distinguished what he called "Abstract or Absolute virtue" from "Practical or Relative virtue." Price said:

> Abstract virtue...denotes what an action is, considered independently of the sense of the agent;...and what, if he judged truly, he would judge he ought to do. --Practical virtue, on the contrary, has a necessary relation to, and dependence upon, the opinion of the agent....It signifies what he ought to do, upon supposition of his having such and such sentiments.[3]

He goes on to say,

> ...for there is a sense in which it may be said, that what any being, in the sincerity of his heart, thinks he ought to do, he indeed ought to do, and would be justly blameable if he omitted to do....[4]

Presumably this holds true for the actions of Rudolph Hoess, the Nazi commandant of Auschwitz, who claimed at his Nuremberg trial that he was doing what at the time he believed was right and his duty. I doubt that Price would relish saying that what Hoess did, "he indeed ought to do." What does it mean to say Hoess' relative or practical duty was to kill thousands of innocent adults and children? Let us

9

grant he thought it was his duty. But it appears
Price must say it <u>was</u> his duty because he thought it
was, not that he merely thought it was, only
"practically and relatively," not "absolutely and
abstractly." On the other hand, if by "it was his
relative duty" Price merely means "he thought it was
his duty," the whole distinction is pointless and
confusing.

People in general have mixed feelings about
this. We all believe that people ought to do the
right thing. Once there is disagreement about what
this is, most people are inclined to say both that
Hoess shouldn't do so-and-so, and that he should do
what he thinks is right, without worrying much about
the consistency of saying both of these things. They
certainly look inconsistent. Suppose a black man
says that everyone ought to do what he believes is
right, and suppose further that there is a deputy
sheriff who believes it is right for him to shoot
black men who go out with white women. If the black
man is known to go out with white women he cannot
escape the logic of the following first person
argument.

> (1) If the sheriff believes that it is
> right for him to perform a certain
> action, then he ought to perform that
> action.
>
> (2) The sheriff believes that it is right
> for him to shoot me.
>
> .'. (3) The sheriff ought to shoot me.

If he also believes that sheriffs ought not to shoot
black men who go out with white women, he contradicts
himself.

It is to escape this contradiction that Price
introduces different senses of "ought" and "right."
In the "relative" sense the sheriff ought to do X
because he believes that he ought in the "absolute"
sense to do X, even though in the "absolute" sense he
ought not to do X. It is impossible for me to
believe that I myself ought to do some particular
action only in the relative sense, for that would be
to disbelieve that I really ought to do it. Saying,

"Some of my obligations are only relative obligations" is like saying, "Some of my beliefs are false": I certainly cannot say which ones are so. Price's distinction is ad hoc, for there is no ground for accepting two different senses of the word "ought" apart from his desire to escape the contradiction.

The alternative to the relativistic reading of "everyone ought to do what he thinks is right" is simply that everyone ought always to be conscientious: The sheriff ought to shoot black men because it is a duty to act on one's moral beliefs. So we seem forced to choose between relativism and inconsistency: The black man, after all, still disagrees with the sheriff, for if you ask him, ought sheriffs to shoot black men who go out with white women, he will answer, "No." The inconsistency in which the black man lands now reduces to a garden variety dilemma: his principles conflict. One principle says it is wrong to shoot people in a certain situation, another principle says it is wrong not to be conscientious, and hence wrong, given the sheriff's beliefs, not to shoot people in that situation. It is clear enough that anyone who accepts the principle that it is always one's duty to be conscientious is going to end up contradicting himself if he has any moral opinions of his own. An obvious solution is to downgrade the conscientiousness principle and deny that everyone ought always to do what he thinks is right; and then there would be no need for Richard Price to propose two different senses of "ought". But it may seem to be very difficult for someone who denies there are moral facts in addition to moral opinions to downgrade the conscientiousness principle.

Well, what would the black man do, as an intelligent non-philosopher, when confronted with the apparent inconsistency? Very likely go back to relativism: "It is right for him but it is wrong for me, that is to say, the sheriff ought to do it, from his point of view, but he ought not, from my point of view."

Philosophers have a special hatred of ethical relativism, a hostility seemingly deeper than their professional hostility to falsehood or a priest's hatred of sin. They have learned to produce ferocious "refutations" of their undergraduates' view (and their social scientist colleagues' view) that something can be right for me and wrong for you. The attacks usually proceed somewhat as follows:

> You say that whatever a person thinks is right _is_ right, _for_ _him_. Surely you wouldn't maintain this with the "for him" left out; for Max thinks dancing is so wicked that it is right to kill anyone who dances, and therefore you would have to agree that it is right, period, to kill dancers. Therefore the "for him" is crucial and the source of whatever appeal this form of ethical relativism has for you. But what does "right for him" mean? Compare "true for him." If you say that whatever a person thinks is true is true, for him, you surely do not mean that "thinking makes it so," that if Max thinks that the world is flat, then, by a telekinetic and geological miracle the world assumes that shape. For someone else may at the same time think the world is not flat, from which we must conclude that the world at time T has contradictory dimensions. No, to say that the world is flat for Max can only mean Max thinks or believes that the world is flat. Otherwise the claim yields gibberish. So too in the case of "right for Max": to claim it is right for Max to kill dancers makes sense if it means that Max _thinks_ or _believes_ it is right to do that. I challenge you to produce another interpretation of "right for him" that does not yield gibberish. But now, if in the original claim we substitute the definition of "for him" that we found, it becomes the following: Whatever a person thinks is right is something he thinks is right. But this is an empty tautology and accepted by everyone, including those who defend absolute and objective morality.

The student is now suitably crushed; he leaves the classroom convinced his philosophy teacher is so clever he can prove truths and falsehoods with equal facility.

But let us look at a presupposition common to this argument and to Price's puzzle. The argument against the "right for him" doctrine subtly assumes the dichotomy "right/believes right" and then easily forces the student to interpret "right for him" to mean "believes right" rather than "right". Thus the student is left with the implied conclusion that while a person might believe an action to be right, the action itself is either right or wrong in a sense that is objective and "absolute" but entirely unexplained. It is easy to show that if "right for me" means "right" relativism is absurd and if "right for me" means "believes right" relativism is trivial; but it is sophistical to claim that one can force upon the "right for me" view either of these reductions. The argument interprets the naive relativist with an uncharitable literalness that makes him choose between saying nothing and proposing a ridiculous test for moral truth. It is question-begging to rule out emotivistic alternatives; and it is insensitive not to explore such alternatives with the relativist rather than assume that he is seeking a method of verification. Our earlier puzzle, "ought a person to do what is right or what he believes is right?," similarly presupposes the "right/believes right" dichotomy. Were it not unfashionable to invent new fallacies, we might call this kind of question-begging the "objectivist fallacy," and say that it is committed when an argument or the statement of a problem simply presupposes that "right" contrasts with "believes right" as "true" contrasts with "believes true." However, I shall bow to fashion and not use the name again (although I might mention it).

When non-philosophers propose ethical relativism it often is difficult to get to the root of what they really mean and it is a cheap shot for philosophers to take them at their literal word. I think that what relativists wish to reject is precisely the "right/believes right" dichotomy. That is, they wish to deny that moral beliefs are truths and falsehoods just like geological beliefs are truths and falsehoods, and this is why they employ the expressions "for me" and "for him" and resist their assimilation

13

to either "right" or "believes right." And if this is so they are not really relativists but emotivists who fumble about trying to escape the objectivist implications of the "right/believes right" dichotomy. If one offers them any reasonably clear version of emotivism they will, with relief, adopt it and abandon the philosophers' formulations of ethical relativism. The "right for me" advocate is not out to establish a method of verifying moral propositions. He does not wish to claim that moral truth can be established as a function of the opinions of either groups or individuals. He wishes to claim that there isn't any moral truth, there is just moral opinion. This is a coherent position, although it may seem to some to be incoherent to claim that moral beliefs and opinions do not divide into true ones and false ones.

Let us return to the case of the black man and the racist sheriff. Having once accepted the view that moral beliefs are attitudes, he might say, "It is right for the sheriff that he do it and it is wrong for me that he do it; but it isn't <u>really</u> right or wrong for either of us; therefore my opinion isn't any better (more justified, closer to the truth) than the sheriff's."

If we want an example of a philosophical confusion that is capable, eventually, of affecting one's attitudes and one's moral life, we have one here. What he is doing is "stepping out of himself" and playing third party, that is to say, adopting the position of an observer who lacks a moral opinion about the sheriff's shooting him. One becomes like a coldly observent anthropologist, which clearly is a mistake when one isn't and instead is personally morally involved. Imagining oneself in the shoes of a third party who has no moral opinion about the matter is like imagining oneself in the shoes of the sheriff who has an opposite moral opinion; one is neither of those persons and it is as though one can need reminding of this fact. I want to say that we can be harmed by promiscuous empathizing with the situations of others, and yet I also want to admit that empathizing is an important part of moral reasoning. A person can be the victim of a peculiar kind of moral anomie that involves viewing his own

14

deepest values and attitudes dispassionately as just another set of values, as though he were someone else.

The symptoms (and probably causes too) of this anomie include the reduction of social morality to "values," a reduction preached by professional educators and social scientists. To these thinkers "values" are personal traits that people have, like pimples, and inappropriate subjects of interpersonal criticism. Another, perhaps more important, cause is unprepared exposure to moral heterogeneity. In this case, timid self-deprecatory allusions to "my value system" and "the sheriff's value system" may have the same kind of basis as the familiar breakdown of tribal values and culture in the face of technological Western culture. What ruins tribal cultures and turns tribesmen to drink is not just violence or job enticements. It is something much subtler that has to do with our innate sociality and the dependence of self worth on affiliation with a social group whose common good, social ethics, and ceremonial trappings retain their vitality and respect. Tribes and American communities can lose their traditional values--in the sense that they no longer take them with sufficient seriousness--because there are now too many apparently well functioning people around who do not share these values at all and pay no serious attention to them. As I shall argue, the things I am for or against on a deep level are taken seriously by me in the way that makes them matters of morality in large part because they have a general appeal and are taken seriously by others around me. Perhaps this is part of why "stepping out of oneself" and looking dispassionately and "objectively" at one's own ethics and the racist sheriff's ethics drains the ethics out of both: One not only confronts heterogeneity but in one's imagination also pulls oneself out of society, on which any live ethics depends, and fancies oneself an asocial, solitary observer.

A system of fundamental, shared social values and morality defines a moral community, within which people can reason and argue on a common basis. If a great many of the people I interact with appear to have a different social morality, and moreover, the possibility of rational adjudication is ridiculed or downplayed, my sense of moral community will be weakened; and then I may come to switch from saying, "This is the way things must be" or "This is what the gods will" to saying "This is just my value system; the sheriff has a different one." If we as a society lose our sense of earnest commitment to a moral community, we may suffer the same fate as those tribes, such as the Ik of Uganda and certain American Indian groups, whose values and traditions withered and decayed. In the case of a tribe we should note that it would be odd to say they discovered their values and traditions to be false. What they first lost was innocence, then respect for what they had, and then their shared ceremonies and practices, all of which are hardly matters of truth and falsity.

The philosopher's quest has been to find the basis for a moral community to which everyone belongs--the universal tribe, as it were, which by definition would not have to face the problem of aliens that has been so debilitating to newly dis- covered jungle tribes. But who (or what) does "everyone" include, and how broad a tribe can one psychologically handle? These are problems that will occupy us later.

The kind of relativist I am discussing is certain that the sheriff shouldn't shoot him, but at the same time denies that his belief is any better than the sheriff's. He feels that if his moral opinion lacks objective status and is a mere personal attitude, it cannot be superior to the sheriff's attitude; it is just one more attitude, on all fours with that of the sheriff. But what constitutes "objective status"? Philosophers in particular may see the problem as a matter of his rejecting moral facts and at the same time believing that morality cannot be the serious and genuine thing it ought to be unless there are moral facts. If I believed there were moral facts or true moral propositions I would indeed be struck by the triviality of the mere biographical fact that I have a moral opposition toward so-and-so.

I am convinced that this is the wrong diagnosis of the sense that one's fundamental values and morality are "mere attitudes" and "no better" than those of anyone else. It is a philosophers' myth that the debilitating loss is the loss of Truth, of conviction that there are moral facts. It is instead a loss of sense of community, of group vitality, cohesiveness, and the authority that a common good creates. What has made people take morality seriously has always been a matter of the authority of the common good of one's tribe, not a matter of confidence in there being true moral propositions. The educated, secular layperson's conception of a "moral absolute" or "moral universal" is almost invariably the idea of a moral principle that is universally accepted.

On the theory I shall be proposing there are no moral facts with which my moral beliefs can contrast and by comparison with which they are trivial. Part of the solution to the relativist's _malaise_ may consist in reminding the man in my example that the sheriff presumably takes his own convictions seriously, and therefore why should not he? Sometimes people speak, in moments of reflection, as though they forgot who they were, or forgot that they too, and not just unreflective sheriffs, belong to a moral community. If the disease has not progressed too far it may remain a Hume's Closet phenomenon, vanishing when the problems of the real world goad them into passionate moral stands.

The irrelevance of moral epistemology to the problem of relativism becomes clearer when we consider some consequences of the loss of religion. What happens when a person ceases to believe that his moral beliefs are grounded in the will of God? Is it that he now thinks they might all be false? If he does, he still believes there is moral truth to be had, for if his own moral beliefs are false then of necessity others are true. He might fear he had lost a reliable source of confirmation, namely God, but he would not have lost everything: morality as a system of truths would remain and he could make educated guesses about right and wrong even if he were denied the omniscient whisperings of God.

Yet merely thinking that one's moral beliefs might be false seems not to be the common reaction. More commonly people say, and sometimes even come to believe, that nothing would be "really" right or wrong, that, as Ivan Karamazov put it, if there is no God then anything is possible. Religious people sometimes express this by saying that if there is no

17

God then all we have are lots of people with different moral opinions, and no one of them can be objectively superior to any other. As a matter of psychological fact, a great many thoughtful people, religious or not, insist on grounding their morality in a source external to themselves and their own feelings. They want to be able to say "it is not just that I feel it is wrong; it _is_ wrong." I think that what people sought, and what they lost when they abandoned God or the gods as the basis of morality, is not truth but a special kind of authority, an authority identical with the homogeneous, stable, confident values of one's tribe, for which the gods were traditional spokesmen and symbols. As a matter of history, morality has been externalized and objectified by being vested wholly in authority: in the authority of one's God, one's tribe, etc. Perhaps one reason for the durability of this conception is that it enables people to pass the responsibility for their moral beliefs and for the consequences of con-scientiously acting on them to God, the Church, the State, the Party, or to What Everybody Thinks. These entities, or those who speak for them, accepted this responsibility and the power that goes with it. Another, more important, reason is that moral autonomy is just too solitary and too frail to ground an effective morality. Autonomy can be noble, something to rise to on occasion, but not something innately social animals can make the primary under-pinning of their moral life.

Traditionally, someone remained responsible for moral beliefs but the responsibility lay with God or one's tribe and did not rest on the backs of individuals. Philosophers perverted this arrangement when they offered their own candidate for the source of moral authority. For they externalized morality by grounding it in The Truth, in true moral proposi-tions or moral facts, for which, of course, nobody is responsible. In this way clever philosophers sought to give Mankind something for nothing; but they outfoxed themselves. The philosophers' procedure succeeds in objectifying morality at the cost of rendering it inaccessible. While we can consult Holy Scripture or received opinion about what is right and free ourselves from a certain kind of responsibility, no one can consult The Truth.

18

This is a principal reason why ethical intuition-ism and non-theological forms of ethical naturalism have never seriously appealed to anyone outside of a handful of professional philosophers, and hence a reason why most modern moral philosophy is not read. These doctrines are impotent as substitutes for God or one's tribe because they offer truths instead of an external authority that one can take for granted and with which one can rest easy. If what people wanted was moral truth, the most they would lose when they replaced God would be a degree of certainty: Someone might err interpreting Holy Scripture but he is more likely to err if he does his own moral truth seeking. This degree of loss does not begin to explain the tendency of people to think that nothing is really right or wrong if morality does not derive from one's God or from the shared beliefs of one's group.

Whether or not grounding morality in divine authority implies there are moral facts depends on one's theology and meta-ethics. If God issued a set of truth-valueless commands such as the Decalogue, this would be all most people would require for there to be an "objective" and "absolute" morality. Those who accepted God's commands could then say that "Thou shalt not kill" is part of "true morality" in the sense that it is a command God issued, but it still would be neither true nor false. One could go on to claim that moral beliefs expressed in the indicative are true when they coincide with one of God's com-mands, for example, by claiming that "Thou shalt not kill" means "God commands you not to kill" or that "Whatever God forbids is wrong" is analytic. To a religious moralist this surely is a case of attempt-ing to gild the lily. As a philosopher and not a religious moralist I shall suggest some intelligible senses in which moral judgments are true or false, although the issue about truth or falsity is basically a minor one.

One need not make meaning claims in order to accept God's will as the foundation of morality, just as a utilitarian does not have to be a definist in order to accept the general happiness as the foundation of morality. Indeed, there is no obstacle to utilitarians and theological moralists being emotivists. However, a crucial difference is that in

19

the case of religious morality the ground is not one's own attitudes but an accepted authority: It is an external and not an internal or autonomous criterion. An implication of the theory I shall defend is that autonomy in Kant's sense is the mark of an inadequate conception of morality and that what we need is heteronomy. If a religious moralist is asked why something is wrong just because God forbids it, he may reply that it is because it is God who forbids it, or he may ask what better reason you could want. When people accept God's authority in morals it is not in the sense in which I accept Roger Tory Peterson as an authority about birds, i.e., as someone who can be relied on to utter truths about birds. I mean that many people accept God's authority in the way a child usually accepts his parents' authority regarding what he is permitted and not permitted to do. If a theological moralist is asked the relatively abstract question, "Is what God forbids wrong?" he may reply "Yes" and go on to say it is a truth that what God forbids is wrong. But it is far from obvious that this is more than a purely honorific use of the word "truth." He may mean only that he accepts God's commands about how he should behave.

Philosophers began to misunderstand how people see the relation of God to morality when Socrates asked Euthyphro whether piety was right because the gods approved of it or whether the gods approved of piety because it was right. For Socrates favored the second alternative and thus initiated the tradition of substituting truth for authority. Insofar as theological moralists believe they must accept either of Socrates' alternatives, the definist alternative usually is more congenial. But they need not claim either that "A is immoral" means "God forbids A," or that it states a fact which God, in his omniscience, knows just as he knows the date on which the sun will explode. When moral sceptics and relativists ask, "Who is to say what is right and wrong," what they seem to mean is, "Who or what can serve as the authority that grounds morality?" If there is no authority, who is to say? Philosophers answer, "Whoever it is that knows." But most skeptics and relativists are not looking for a person who knows something, they are looking for a person or entity whose saying so suffices; what they are interested in

20

is its nature and status, not its knowledge.

As religious morality is questioned and close knit, homogeneous cultures look around themselves and begin to feel self-conscious, relativism, rational egoism, and various crank systems of philosophy and religion gain more adherents. What one observes are heroic individualists who attempt to "go it alone" in their moral and spiritual lives and much larger numbers of people who crave moral community and commit themselves to the potentially sinister authority of cults and leaders rather than to the natural authority of a common or community good. In the West this is a consequence of excessive individualism with its attendant moral autonomy and its idea of a purely commercial relation between individuals and society. What causes moral crisis is that whereas political and economic individualism is possible, and consciously cultivated in America, moral individualism is not possible. People who have not understood this--the American "individualists-gone-mad" common during the past two decades--preached dogmas and made policies that were destructive of our sense of belonging to moral communities.

One thing I have been doing in this chapter is attempting to rebut the charge that the denial of moral facts corrupts the youth, by finding different and more plausible villains. Amoralism and relativism are not consequences of the denial of moral facts. They instead are a consequence of loss of confidence in the interpersonal acceptance and reliability of values and moral beliefs and, for some people, loss of belief in God as the guarantor of interpersonal acceptability.

Chapter I: NOTES

1. Charles   Stevenson,   ETHICS   AND   LANGUAGE   (New
    Haven: Yale Univerity Press, 1944).

2. Gilbert   Harman,   THE   NATURE   OF   MORALITY   (New
    York: Oxford   University   Press,   1977),   Chapter
    One.

3. Richard Price, REVIEW OF THE PRINCIPLE QUESTIONS
    IN MORALS (London, Oxford University Press, 1978)
    p. 177.

4. Op. Cit., pp. 177-178.

II.   MORALS AS PASSIONS

2.1 <u>Emoting, Exclaiming, and Asserting.</u> When
we ask "What does 'good' mean?" we may mean any of
several things.   (1) We may be asking for a
definition of the sort dictionaries give, in which
case we turn to the dictionary.   (2) In moral
discussions and arguments people often say, "What do
you mean by 'good' here?," or, "It depends on what
you mean by 'good'." Here I am being asked for my
reasons, for features or circumstances of the thing
in virtue of which I call it good.   In this sense
the meaning is identical with what Richard Hare has
called the "descriptive meaning" of "good."[1]   This
is what most people want when they ask what "good"
means, although it seldom is what philosophers want.
(3) We may be asking for a synonym or synonymous
expression.   This   is   one   type   of   dictionary
definition, although it is not how dictionaries
define "good."   Partial and incomplete definitions
are possible such as "praiseworthy" and "commend-
able," but these are trivial.

(4) We may be asking for an explanation of how
the word is used. If some normative words are more
like "bravo" or "hello" than like "triangle" or
"butterfly," we must use rather than mention words
in our explanations of them.   No one knows the
legitimate boundaries of such explanations.   That
is, facts about how a normative word is used might
begin as part of an account of meaning and
imperceptibly shade off into other generalizations
which, while enlightening, are not part of an
explanation of meaning. But this shift is in any
case not very important, not only because no one can
say what a sharp boundary to an explanation of the
meaning of normative words and sentences would be
like, but also because exclusive preoccupation with
meaning trivializes what philosophers say about
normative language.   I suspect that it is a mistake
even to look for a boundary between the empirical
and the "conceptual" in this kind of case, and that
in any event the empirical is as illuminating as the
conceptual.

Some philosophers maintained that words such as "good," "bad," "right," "wrong" and "ought" are, in themselves, persuasive devices. But people seldom are much influenced by the use of these words. They are poor instruments with which to attempt to alter the attitudes of adults; in the case of small children it may be a different matter. If Harry tells me that some action would be wrong, he thereby communicates to me that he is opposed to it, which by itself doesn't move me at all. If I am persuaded by what Harry says, I am not persuaded by being told that it is wrong but by being told what is wrong with it, that is, by being given a reason that allows me to classify the act as a kind I already think is wrong. What persuades me is the linkage that is forged with my pre-existing moral beliefs and not the laudatory or imperative "force" of the moral words. Unsupported moral judgments probably have greater influence in morally homogeneous societies than they do in America, but even in a morally homogeneous society it is not the laudatory or imperative "force" of the word that persuades but the confidence people in such a society have that if someone calls something immoral then almost everyone else including the highest moral authorities would also call it immoral.

Very often, when someone makes a moral pronouncement he knows perfectly well that his listener already agrees with him. So there is no question of his trying to influence him. What, then, is he doing? Perhaps he is expressing his feelings or attitudes, but it makes no sense to say he is trying to induce similar attitudes in another.

Similar criticisms apply to the theory that moral judgments are imperatives or contain imperatives as an element of their meaning. In general, imperatives are issued because the person who issues them wants the person to whom he issues them to do something, counterexamples about bored drill sergeants notwithstanding. They are attempts to bring about action, though certainly not by persuasion, in situations involving emergency, authority, or unequal social relationship. But when I tell you my moral opinion I seldom want you to do anything, although I may want you to believe as I do. And I do not want even the latter if I know that you already agree with me. I am not issuing orders to you, first because I seldom am in the requisite social position to issue any orders to you; second, because it would be rude; and third, because I know there is not the slightest reason why you, as an adult and an equal, should pay any attention to them.

We sometimes write declarative sentences in an "imperative" way, that is, with an exclamation point at the end, and sometimes say them this way too. Here the aim is emphasis, not the issuance of commands. In moral arguments, more often than in factual arguments, we deliver our judgments with heat and indignation, in other words as exclamations. It is on just these occasions that we are most anxious to force the other person to agree with us. But it would be as much a mistake to think, when we are striving to persuade and we exclaim, "But abortion is immoral!," that this utterance is or contains an imperative, as it would be to think in an argument of similar intensity, that "But it does rain little frogs in Mississippi!" is or contains an imperative. If a person is out to persuade me of something, that is a fact about him, not a fact about the function or meaning of the words he uses.

Are there moral feelings and moral emotions? Usually, when someone makes a sincere moral judgment, what he feels or is aware of is pretty much the kind of thing he is aware of when he makes any other kind of utterance: he is aware of the words (whether he says them aloud or merely thinks them), and the words and their organization are familiar and unsurprising in a way that assures him he knows the words and is not talking gibberish. The feelings that sometimes do accompany our moral judgments—anger, contempt, sympathy, concern, admiration, hatred, worry, indignation, dislike, and so on—, arise in other circumstances too. There is nothing peculiarly moral about them.

Consider exclamatory words and sentences as a model for understanding moral words and sentences. Suppose that we wish to discover the meaning of "Help!" Adolph is rapidly sinking into quicksand and he shouts "Help!" An attempt at a definition might go as follows: "'Help' (said by Adolph) means

'Adolph desires (or is expressing an urgent desire for) assistance.'" Now it undoubtedly is true that Adolph is expressing an urgent desire for assistance, but because the definition equates an exclamation with a declarative sentence, it is hopeless. Moreover, Adolph, while about to go under, would be loathe to replace the one expression with the other and shout "Adolph is expressing an urgent desire for assistance!" If Adolph says that, the correct response is, "No you aren't."

THE RANDOM HOUSE DICTIONARY offers an alternative to straightforward definition: "help--interj... (used as an exclamation to call for assistance or to attract attention.)"[2] But suppose that Freda says, "If Adolph shouts for help, ignore him." Freda is not exclaiming or calling for assistance. Assuming we are dealing with a single meaning of the word, we appear to have a dilemma: On the one hand, the dictionary entry is a plausible account of "Help!", shouted from the quicksand, but an incorrect account of "If Adolph shouts for help, ignore him." On the other hand, if we adopt the definition by synonymous expressions we have a plausible definition of "help" in "If Adolph shouts for help, ignore him," but an incorrect definition of a shout from the quicksand.

Let us intuitively divide sentences containing the word "help," in its emergency call sense, into exclamatory and nonexclamatory ones. Thus "Help!" is an exclamatory "help"-sentence and "Adolph called for help" is a nonexclamatory "help"-sentence. I define the nonexclamatory sentence "Adolph called for help" as "Adolph called for assistance or to attract attention." Here we mention two sentences and claim they have the same meaning. I explain the exclamatory sentence by saying that it is an exclamation used to call for assistance or to attract attention. The same words are used in explaining the exclamatory sentence as are mentioned in defining the nonexclamatory sentence, namely, calling for assistance or to attract attention. This is evidence that the definition and the explanation, taken together, give <u>one</u> meaning of "help": The occurrence of the same expression in both cases distinguishes this meaning of "help" from other meanings, as in "hired help." What we end up with is an "emotivist" account of exclamatory uses of "help" together with a "subjectivist" definition of nonexclamatory uses of "help." I shall argue for a similar two-part account of normative words.

Part of the problem with exclamations is identifying exactly what it is that is supposed to have a meaning. The definition of "triangle," by long standing and generally unobjectionable convention, attributes a meaning to the word type "triangle." But when we explain that "Help!" is a call for assistance, we cannot seriously claim that we have stated a truth about a word type. The type "Help!" is not and does not mean a call for assistance. Some persons's shouting a token of "help" (in the appropriate circumstances) is a call for assistance.

Nondescriptivist explanations of the meaning of spoken or written moral judgments similarly must refer to actions of individual persons. If an analysis of "Abortion is immoral" contains the prescription "Let there be no abortions," the latter expression makes sense only as referring to individual acts of prescribing. Contrast this with the analysis, "Abortion has disutility," which only concerns two propositions claimed to have the same meaning and does not refer to the actions or tokenings of individual persons. Emotivist and prescriptivist analyses attempt to get at the meaning of "immoral" by reference to the actions of individuals. In doing so such theories do not explain what "x is wrong" means; they instead explain what a person's calling x wrong means, in terms of doing other things such as prescribing or commanding.

2.2 A Dispositional Theory. I want to distinguish judgmental from nonjudgmental moral sentences much as I distinguished exclamatory from nonexclamatory uses of "help." Then I will be in a position to provide separate accounts of each and, as in the case of exclamations, argue that although the two accounts are different, they complement one another and together provide a unitary account of what we mean when we use moral words. But a new element will be introduced: the notion of a moral belief. I shall show that a moral belief is best understood

27

as a particular kind of disposition, and then explain both "Abortion is immoral" (said by Harry) and "Harry thinks abortion is immoral" in terms of their relations to a moral belief. This will strengthen the claim that "immoral" has a single meaning in its judgmental and nonjudgmental uses.

The emotivists failed to come up with a theory that explained judgmental sentences such as "Abortion is immoral" and also nonjudgmental sentences such as "Harry thinks abortion is immoral." For example, they claimed that "ought" sentences express attitudes, give commands, or issue prescriptions. These theories may have some slight plausibility as theories about the meaning of "Harry ought to vote against the bill," but they fail as accounts of the meaning of "Harry thinks he ought to vote against the bill." "Abortion is immoral" might, with superficial plausibility, be rendered as "Don't anybody abort". But if I instead say, "If I thought abortion were immoral I would vote against the bill," I am not expressing an attitude, commanding, or issuing a prescription, for the same kind of reason that Freda is not giving a call for assistance when she says, "If I were in the quick-sand like Adolph over there I would shout 'Help!' too." The emotivists only explained someone's calling something immoral, or right, or wrong. It is not merely that "Harry thinks A is immoral" lacks the "emotive element," it also says something the emotivist analysis leaves out. For it attributes a moral belief to someone and an adequate ethical theory should explain moral beliefs and not restrict itself to the analysis of sentences.

The mistake I am ascribing to imperative, emotivist, and prescriptivist analyses of the meaning of moral words is somewhat like what John Searle calls the speech act fallacy.[3] A speech act analysis, Searle says, has the pattern: "The word W is used to perform speech act A," an example of which is Hare's claim that the word "good" is used to commend. Searle says that such analyses are meant to explain, at least in part, the meaning of W, and also that an analogy is intended with so-called performative verbs: "Just as 'promise' is used to make promises, and 'bet' to make bets, so they argued 'good' is used to commend, and 'true' is used to endorse, ect." The speech act analysis is easily refuted, Searle says, because there are countless literal uses of "good," as in questions, conditionals, and so on, in which it is not used to commend:

> Calling something good is characteristical-ly praising or commending or recommending it, etc. But it is a fallacy to infer from this that the meaning of "good" is explain-ed by saying it is used to perform the act of commendation. And we demonstrate that it is a fallacy by showing that there are an indefinite number of counter-examples of sentences where "good" has a literal occur-rence yet where the literal utterances of the sentences are not performances of the speech act of commendation....[4]

There is also a "sophisticated form" of the speech act fallacy, Searle says:

> Often the speech act analysts qualified their statements of the form "W is used to perform act A" by saying that the primary use of W is to perform act A. They were thus not committed to the view that every literal utterance of W is a performance of act A, but rather that utterances which are not performances of the act have to be explained in terms of utterances which are.[5]

Searle's "sophisticated" speech act analyst must do this because he wants to claim that "good" has the same meaning in moral judgments and in conditional and interrogative moral sentences, even though "good" is not being used to perform speech act A in the latter. So he claims that reports about Harry's moral utterance report speech act A, hypothetical moral sentences hypothesize the speech act, moral questions ask if speech act A will occur (has occurred, or is occurring). Searle says that this will not work and gives a number of counterexamples.

My theory avoids the crude form of the speech act fallacy by giving different accounts of judgmen-tal and nonjudgmental uses of moral words. But it might be thought to commit the sophisticated form because I maintain that nonjudgmental moral sentences affirm, question, or hypothesize the dispositions that judgmental sentences manifest, somewhat as, according to Searle's account of a sophisticated speech act theory, nonjudgmental moral sentences affirm, hypothesize, and ask about speech acts. We must see whether or not my own theory is subject to counterexamples. There are two general reasons why Searle's criticism of the sophisticated speech act analysis does not apply to my view. First, nonjudgmental moral sentences are not about speech acts but about the moral beliefs moral judgments express. Second, the paraphrases I will offer of nonjudgmental moral sentences are only partial definitions. For in every paraphrase of a conditional or interrogative moral sentence, we must suppose that the opposition (or support) the sentence is about bears what I will call the marks of the moral. Otherwise it will not be <u>moral</u> opposition or support. But we are getting ahead of the narrative. More of my own view needs to be laid out before we can see whether or not it is subject to Searle-type counterexamples.

Someone's believing theft is wrong is identical with his having a certain kind of opposition disposition regarding theft. In saying "Theft is wrong" he putatively manifests this disposition: He emits normative behavior. Thus, saying "Theft is wrong" or "I ought not to steal" is opposing theft just as is resisting temptation to steal or punishing thieves. If Harry believes the soprano gave a good performance, he may express his belief by saying "That was a good performance," shouting "Bravo!", presenting the soprano with roses, or feeling pleased. Valuing something or thinking it right is not entertaining a proposition but being disposed to support it, and this support can be both verbal and nonverbal. If Harry believes that A is immoral, then the disposition is his being opposed to A: he is ill-disposed toward it. What putatively manifests and is evidence for that disposition is his relevant normative behavior, which includes the words he utters. So the theory maintains that sincere normative utterances are conventionalized normative behavior, very much as, on Wittgenstein's view, saying "I am in pain" is conventionalized pain behavior.

Nonjudgmental moral sentences do not express moral dispositions but are about them or their manifestations. Consequently they are fact stating if declarative and can be paraphrased in the manner of subjectivistic definism. The paraphrases I will suggest are just schemas for definitions because we have yet to distinguish moral from nonmoral opposition.

What follows are a few sample paraphrases of (a) attributions of moral beliefs, (b) attributions of moral utterances, (c) conditional moral sentences, and (d) moral questions. Only the first three, of course, will have truth values. Within each kind we must distinguish first person sentences from the less-difficult-to-paraphrase third person sentences. I will for convenience call the disposition opposition. In some cases disapproval, hatred, fear, or contempt may be more accurate than opposition, in other cases a combination of these. Favorable moral beliefs will be characterizable under a wide range of positive attitudes.

(a) Attributions of moral beliefs: To begin with a nonmoral case, "Harry thinks the picture is bad" means "Harry doesn't like the picture," but given different beliefs of the speaker it could mean "Harry thinks that most critics, or most thoughtful observers, would not like the picture." "Harry believes abortion is immoral" means "Harry is opposed to abortion," in other words, it asserts that Harry has the disposition of which "Abortion is immoral" (said by Harry) would be a manifestation. "Harry thinks he ought to pay his debt to Freda" means "Harry is opposed to his not paying his debt to Freda." What "Harry thinks war is evil" means will depend in part on the kinds of reasons he has, that is to say, on the aspects of war which lead him to morally condemn it. If he thinks war is merely stupid and wasteful, then "Harry thinks war is evil" ("bad" might be the better word here) probably means "Harry opposes and has contempt for war"; but if he thinks it is brutal and unjust then his opposition will be stronger and he will also hate it. "I used to think W was immoral" means "I used to be opposed to W."

(b) Attributions of moral utterances: Sentences about what someone _says_ is immoral are not about a disposition but about a person's putative manifestation of a disposition. Thus, "Freda said that A is immoral," as well as "Freda said 'A is immoral'," mean "Freda uttered a sentence which putatively manifested opposition to A." "I said that A is immoral" can be taken normatively or reportively: As a report, it means "I (putatively) demonstrated opposition to A"; this is the interpretation appropriate when I do not or no longer believe that A is immoral. On the reiterative or emphatic interpretation it is interchangeable with "A is immoral."

(c) Conditional moral sentences: Neither the antecedent nor the consequent of a moral conditional expresses a moral stand of the speaker, though each might if it were detached. Consequently I interpret both the antecedent and the consequent as fact stating and nonjudgmental. "If Harry thought A was immoral he would vote against the bill" means "If Harry was opposed to A he would vote against the bill." "If Harry ought to do it then I ought to help" could mean, "If I knew that Harry was opposed to his not doing it, then I would be opposed to my not helping"; more commonly it means "If I were to be opposed to Harry's not doing it, then I would be opposed to my not helping."

First person conditionals are interpreted to attribute the relevant disposition to the speaker. Some attribute possible future dispositions to oneself, as in "If A is immoral I shall vote against the bill," which I paraphrase as "If I were to come to be opposed to A then I would vote against the bill." Others simply hypothesize nonactual dispositions, as in "If A were immoral I would vote against the bill," which I paraphrase as "If I were opposed to A I would vote against the bill."

I am suggesting that the only interpretations of conditional moral sentences we accept are ones in which the moral clauses refer to dispositions of actual or imagined persons. With this in mind consider "If abortion is immoral then it is odd that it is legal."[6] The example poses a difficulty because no one is indicated as the person who has or is imagined to have the disposition. Nevertheless

32

there are some plausible interpretations. If what the speaker has in mind is that he expects law to follow popular moral opinion, then his sentence means, "If most people are opposed to abortion it is odd that it is legal." On this interpretation the sentence rings true. A more natural interpretation allows the paraphrase, "If most reasonable people would be opposed to abortion if they knew the facts, it is odd that it is legal." On this interpretation the sentence sounds false; this probably is the correct one since the original sentence also sounds false.

(d) Moral questions: Third person questions involve nothing new, but first person questions are less straightforward. "Does Freda think A is immoral" means "Is Freda opposed to A?" But it seems counterintuitive to render "Is A immoral?" as "Am I opposed to A?" because the first question calls for decision and judgment, whereas the second appears to call only for psychological investigation. But "Am I opposed to A?" need not be a psychological question; it can itself be viewed as calling for decision and judgment. The point is that "Is A immoral?" is not a question about my present moral beliefs but is about the possible reasons for future moral beliefs I might have. Hence a plausible interpretation is, "Are there facts such that were I to know them I would be opposed to A?" Alternatively, however, we can interpret "Is A immoral?" as quasi-normative in the sense that it may indicate vacillation between the belief that A is immoral and the belief that it is not. On this interpretation the question indicates the absence of a relevant moral disposition together with the desire to acquire one.

We need to say something about these "dispositions" that I claim moral beliefs really are. Suppose that Freda believes that race discrimination is wrong. This means that Freda is opposed to things she recognizes as race discrimination. On the one hand, we might define her disposition in terms of its causal basis; on the other, the evidence for her disposition consists of her verbal and nonverbal behavior and we might define her disposition in terms of this behavior. These are two competing candidates, a causal one and a

33

behavioral one, for what a (moral) disposition
essentially is.

How could we determine the causal basis? We can
hypothesize neural and environmental causes of her
emitting a particular pattern of behavior against
race discrimination. In the case of made-up
examples we can hypothesize anything we want; but we
can do little more than speculate about the causes
of an actual moral disposition. I assume that a
moral disposition has causes, but since nobody knows
what they are we cannot use them to infer which bits
of behavior count as manifestations of Freda's
opposition.

The situation is different when we can pinpoint
the cause. Appendicitis has symptoms which are
sometimes difficult to distinguish from the symptoms
of different ailments. Physicians, once having
identified an inflamed appendix as the cause of what
hitherto was only a loosely connected group of
symptoms, can admit or reject a patient's symptoms
as manifestations of appendicitis according as they
are or are not caused by an inflamed appendix. But
in the case of a person's disposition to oppose
something we lack such exact causal knowledge. Word
meanings and conventions, not knowledge of causes,
tell us if a given bit of Freda's behavior is a
manifestation of her opposition to race discrimination. Hence there wouldn't be much use, given the
present state of knowledge about causes of human
behavior, in defining a moral disposition in terms
of its causal basis.

It is conceivable that future scientists will
become so skillful at identifying such causes that
they, and perhaps people in general, will define
dispositions in terms of them. If so we could claim
that Freda was morally opposed to race discrimination because her brain was in a certain state, even
though she did not emit the behavior we now accept
as necessary for having the disposition. Such a
barely conceivable scientific advance would bring
about a corresponding conceptual change. For as
things stand today, her behavior not only is evidence, it also is constitutive of the disposition in
the sense that our conception of this behavior is
part of what we mean when we say she is opposed to

so-and-so.   Hence   Freda's   opposition   behavior
constitutes   what   Wittgensteinians   called   criteria
for her having such-and-such an opposition.   If the
scientific   advances   I   mentioned   were   actually   to
take place, this behavior would get demoted from
criteria to symptoms.

There are borderline cases of being opposed to
something,   cases   in   which   evidence   for   a   person's
opposition   is   balanced   by   contrary   evidence.   This
also holds for the subclass of oppositions we call
moral oppositions and requires us to admit borderline cases of someone's having a moral belief.   It
also tells us that moral beliefs admit of degrees of
strength or intensity, this being a function of the
strength   and   threshold   of   a   person's   opposition
behavior.

Another consequence of the dispositional theory
is if someone believes race discrimination is wrong
he is disposed to oppose it.   One obvious way is
refraining   from   race   discrimination.   So,   in   general, what he is disposed to do includes doing the
things he believes are right and forebearing doing
the things he believes are wrong.   In this very
important respect moral beliefs are not different
from ordinary likes and aversions.   If Max dislikes
air travel we expect him to manifest this disposition by refusing to fly; but he may fly anyway, and
if he does, we expect him not to enjoy it, or to
complain about it.   It is as natural a consequence
of a person's moral beliefs that he in general
refrains or tries to refrain from doing what he
believes is wrong, as it is a consequence of dis-
liking air travel that someone refrains or tries to
refrain from flying.   On the theory it is an equally
natural   consequence   that   sometimes   he   does   not
refrain.   But we should remember that people almost
always do what they think is right and forebear
doing what they think is wrong when it is easy, and
that when they habitually do otherwise we begin to
doubt their words.

As   David   Hume   enjoyed   pointing   out   in   the
TREATISE,   moral   intellectualists   have   difficulty
bridging the gap between a person's accepting a
moral proposition and his having a motive for
heeding it.   This is the first of two problems about

the connection between moral belief and action that any adequate ethical theory must be able to solve: How does moral belief motivate us? The second, strangely enough, is, How can moral belief fail to motivate us? How moral beliefs supply motives cannot be a problem for the theory I am presenting, for if a person actually is opposed to doing something, it is tautologous to go on to claim that he has a motive for not doing it. Indeed, according to the theory, just saying sincerely that race discrimination is immoral is already a case of being moved to action. Now, if moral utterances are a species of moral action, we should expect them to be praised, blamed, and excused just as are nonverbal actions. And indeed they are. We often get as indignant about a person's beliefs as we do about the behavior they sanction. However, what someone says usually elicits less condemnation or admiration than nonverbal behavior, for the obvious reason that many things hurt us more than words.

The second problem about belief and action that the theory solves concerns weakness of will and related matters. How can a person behave contrary to her own moral beliefs? Almost equally interest- ing, how can she behave as though she had a moral belief she in fact does not have? Suppose that Freda consistently says race discrimination is wrong and unfair; in general she is fair and friendly toward black people, gets indignant at racists, speaks up for equal opportunity legislation, and so on. This usually would be sufficient evidence that she is morally opposed to race discrimination. Now suppose she refuses to sell her house to a black person and we have good evidence that she did this because of pressure from her colleagues and neighbors. By itself, her refusal to sell at her asking price is evidence that she is not morally opposed to race discrimination. But in the face of all her contrary behavior we instead call it weakness of will. If the moral belief is the disposition, and the disposition continues to exist when she acts contrariwise out of fear or tempta- tion, then so does the moral belief continue to exist. It is not different from being a cigaret smoker who refrains on occasion, out of fear or social pressure, and yet still warrants the descrip- tion "cigaret smoker."

The explanation we can give of weak will, as the occasional defeats our tendencies or dispositions meet, is not available to prescriptivist theories such as Richard Hare's. If, all things considered, I prescribe an act, it is indeed puzzling if I do not do it, and such a theory must fall back on the view that, in some sense, I cannot do it.[7] But my theory does not say I prescribe or will every act I think I ought to perform. It says I am in favor of them and hence that I will perform such actions unless some other moral or nonmoral want prevails. I am disposed to be fair, but I am also disposed to tend to my bank account. If fairness costs me money and I opt for my money, I may believe I did wrong even while doing it. A moral disposition can compete with egoism, group egoism, and various passions, and sometimes it loses.

If someone persists in discriminatory practices, eventually we will not know whether he acts contrary to his own moral beliefs or no longer believes race discrimination is wrong. Sometimes what one says outweighs the evidence of actions and convinces us he thinks it is wrong, other times actions outweigh the evidence of his words. We call the first kind of situation wickedness or weakness of will, and the second lying or self-deception. There is a simple reason why a person's saying that a certain action would be immoral often is better evidence for what he believes than what he does. Talk is cheap, it is a less expensive and therefore more sensitive barometer of weak opposition to, say, promise breaking than is keeping promises. Actually keeping one's promises is more likely to cost a person other things he wants.

We saw that the moral opinions people deliver in quiet conversation among friends are most implausibly construed as orders, prescriptions, or persuasive devices of any sort. The primary function of saying that something is wrong is exactly what at first sight it appears to be, namely informing others. I am not ordering, prescribing or venting emotions, but communicating my moral or evaluative opinion. But it is not by magic or induction that you know I morally oppose what I call wrong, as though my utterance had to be a mere clue since it is not a moral proposition. When I call something

37

wrong I intentionally communicate my moral opposition to the hearer or reader, just as when I shout
"Bravo!" I intend to communicate my liking of the
concert. Speaker and hearer learn these purposes
when they learn the use of these words. And if they
do, then the hearer does not infer my opposition any
more than people in general understand ordinary
conversation by inference or induction. If someone
says to me, "I am going to the store," and I conclude that she is telling me she is going to the
store, inference plays no greater or lesser role
here than it does when she tells me A is immoral.

If my saying, "It would be wrong to do so-and-
so" serves primarily to communicate my opposition,
why do I not simply assert I am opposed to doing
so-and-so? One reason is that not all opposition is
moral opposition. Another reason is that my utterance, "It would be wrong to do it," is the best way
verbally to communicate my disposition. How could
there by any better evidence of my opposition than
an actual demonstration of it? If I wish to show I
am opposed, I do best by opposing it, which is what
I am doing in saying it would be wrong as distinct
from merely claiming that I am opposed. It is a
case of actions speaking louder than propositions.
I think this has always been recognized as one of
the strengths (whatever the defects) of the emotivist theory of ethics. Saying "I have an opposition
disposition toward race discrimination" is like
saying, "How amusing," dead-pan, in response to a
hilarious joke. "It would be wrong" stands to "I
have an opposition disposition toward it" much as
laughing stands to saying "That joke is funny." This
is not to say that "It would be wrong," in contrast
to "I am oppposed to it," infallibly indicates one's
opposition. A laugh or a shout of "Bravo!" can be
simulated or insincere, and so can, "It would be
wrong to do it." Nonetheless, a laugh is a superior
mode of communicating amusement than is saying "I am
amused."

2.3 <u>Values and Truths.</u> Subjective relativism,
other forms of definism, and intuitionism all claim
that moral judgments are fact stating and therefore
literally truths or falsehoods. Each of these
theories substitutes for my moral beliefs or your
moral beliefs or Freda's moral beliefs, moral

propositions which need not be anybody's moral beliefs and then proceeds to lay down truth conditions for them. This whole approach is wrong because it confuses a mode of behavior with a set of propositions. What counts against the view that moral claims assert facts is the objectivity and impersonality of truth itself and not merely the difficulty of verification. Valuing is something I do like laughing or fighting. My valuing things, morally condemning things, and so on, are, together with my reasons, what constitute my moral life and they differ from but overlap and merge with my loves and hates, likes and aversions.

Suppose I were to claim that my loving a woman was true or false. I do not mean that it is true or false that I love a woman, but that the loving itself was true or false and its truth or falsity was the only important thing about my love. As evidence I might point out that we do, after all, speak of true love and false love, as well as foolish love. Suppose, moreover, we had a locution that lent additional credence to this hypothesis: Saying "Loves Mary" was a way of verbally expressing love which, unlike "I love Mary," could never be construed as an autobiographical report. Thus, "Loves Mary," together with "I love Mary," gave us a pair of love-sentences analogous to the pair, "The humpback whale ought to be saved" and "I believe the humpback whale ought to be saved." We can imagine that someone would prefer "Loves Mary" to "I love Mary" when he wished to manifest his love--i.e., to actually engage in loving--rather than report that he has this disposition toward Mary, just as he would prefer "The humpback whale ought to be saved" to "I believe the humpback whale ought to be saved" when he has the same kind of contrast in mind. He might on many occasions use "Loves Mary" and "I love Mary" interchangeably, just as we often use "A is wrong" and "I believe A is wrong" interchangeably, but there will be occasions when he finds one of them more appropriate than the other.

Now imagine that a philosopher writes "Loves Mary" on the board and proceeds to search out its meaning. Since people say "Loves Mary" meaningfully it ought to be possible to say what it means; he does know that sometimes it is used interchangeably with "I love Mary." He decides that it is either true or not true, while admitting that it might be extremely difficult to determine which. He notes that "Loves Mary" is intersubjective and only affirms the loving of Mary, whereas "I love Mary" is a subjective report. If "Loves Mary" is true, it is not true "for me" or "for you," indeed its truth or falsity has nothing to do with whether you or I happen to have certain feelings toward Mary. It might be true that I love Mary, but false that loves Mary, in which case my loving Mary is mistaken, that is to say, I love Mary erroneously. Similarly, it may be true that loves Mary and false that I love Mary, indeed it may be false that anybody loves Mary, just as, our philosopher claims, it might be true that dancing is immoral but false that anybody thinks it is immoral. We could imagine that "Loves Mary" is true and "Loves John" is false, notwithstanding that nobody loves Mary and everybody loves John; thus Mary would indeed be blessed and could despise John for enjoying false love.

Whole schools of love-objectivists could arise. There would be ideal observers who maintain that "Loves Mary" is true if Mary is lovable, i.e., the sort of woman whom any perfectly rational, disinterested, dispassionate, omniscient, observer would love. Tough-minded intuitionists would argue that there are no defining conditions for the truth of "Loves Mary" and that everybody might love Mary and all do so erroneously; they would do battle with tender-minded subjective relativists who claim that "Loves Mary" means the same as the subjective report, "I love Mary." And of course, there would be emotivists who deny any propositional status to "Loves Mary" while claiming that "I love Mary" is an autobiographical report. All, with the exception of the emotivists, would hope that advances in amorous science would determine whether "Loves Mary," "Loves John," etc., were true or false, and thus settle the momentous question of whether or not their loving Mary or John was erroneous.

Moves of these kinds make as much sense about morality as they do about love and hate. "Abortion is immoral," by itself and when it is not the manifestation of any person's moral belief, is just a sentence that could have a moral use but which, standing by itself on a philosopher's blackboard, has no moral use; to say it is true or false in the same literal sense in which "Harry thinks abortion is immoral" is true or false is like saying that the loving of Mary is true or false independently of whether anyone loves Mary. There is no love unless there is somebody who loves, there is no value unless there is somebody who values. The sense in which right, wrong, and value exist, and expressions of them exist, is most nearly akin to the sense in which there exist love and expressions of love. Nonetheless, if valuing is something we do, then like anything else we do it can be appraised according as it is done well or poorly.

The question whether moral judgments can be true or false is not a simple one, but neither is it very important (which means it will not get a thorough treatment). The mistake would be to use the denial of truth value as an argument, for example, as an argument for why many moral disagreements are intractable, or for rejecting intuitionism and definism. This would be to go about things back-wards, for the question of whether moral judgments have truth values depends on one's theory and is not independently decidable. The important task, the one that must come first, is to develop a positive theory of the nature of moral beliefs and the function of moral sentences. Then we should see what we can say about truth and falsity in the light of the theory.

On the theory I am proposing we can go either way: there are a number of situations in which it would not be wrong or bizarre to call moral judg-ments true or false. Often people call moral claims false because they are ignorant ones, that is, based on false factual beliefs or logical errors. Very commonly, when someone insists that a moral belief is false, he has reasons for rejecting it that he expects rational people would accept as good reasons if they came to know and understand them. In these kinds of cases the speaker's charge of falsehood can be correct in the sense that the moral claim may indeed be ignorant, or his reasons would in fact be accepted by rational people. Sometimes however, the use of "true" and "false" seems purely emphatic, as when a person speaks of deeply felt or ultimate moral principles as basic moral truths. In this kind of case we do not say that the moral claim is true unless we agree with the speaker, but in any event, we understand this use of "true." I do not insist that these are what most people mean when they call moral claims true or false, only that they are plausible grounds for using "true" and "false" that are consistent with the theory.

From a philosophical point of view the interpretation that says moral claims are neither true nor false is at least as interesting as the interpretation that says moral claims <u>are</u> true or false. The latter ultimately depends on the fact that most people have similar deep wants and aversions and hence can be predicted to agree morally when they agree about the facts, about logic, and have had some similar experiences. It is largely the attainability of substantial agreement under similar conditions that moves us to count moral beliefs among the true and the false. But this is not, I think, a matter simply to be discovered but a matter of interpretive choice. The similarity of moral beliefs to loves and hates, likes and aversions, and the ways they contrast with ordinary descriptive beliefs, invite the denial of truth value. We can claim that moral beliefs lack truth values because they are dispositions, they are such things as oppositions and approvals; they are, to paraphrase Hume, original facts, complete in themselves.[8] We can maintain that moral judgments lack truth value because they are behavior, they are expressions of these dispositions. We are not driven to calling moral beliefs truths and falsehoods just because they can satisfy various criteria of rationality. Some moral beliefs are ignorant ones, but it is a further theoretical step to call them false because they are ignorant; perhaps it is damning enough for any argumentative or pedagogical purpose to point out that a moral belief is ignorant.

What I am saying is that while we can legitimately call moral judgments and beliefs true or false, nevertheless if we accept the positive theory I am proposing there is little incentive for doing so except in casual and colloquial contexts. Consider an analogoy with aesthetics. People who are interested in the arts are more likely when they are

very young than when they are older to argue that
aesthetic judgments are objectively true or false.
It is much more often a characteristic of the bright
and young to argue that it is a brute fact that The
Archduke Trio is better than How Much is That Doggie
in the Window. I think that as one grows older and
becomes more self-confident about one's tastes, the
relevance of whether or not there exists such a
brute fact vanishes. The older person can say
something about why he likes the Beethoven better
than the juke box song, he is sure there is some
correlation between intelligence and education and
these preferences; but he is more likely to let it
go at that. It is as though when a person has not
yet made his musical tastes comfortably part of
himself, when he still feels a twinge of concern
that he may be following a herd, a fad or a conceit,
that he reaches out for support in the form of
aesthetic facts. This self-confidence I speak of is
not pigheadedness, it is a kind of self-knowledge.
At this stage it simply does not matter that there
are no objective aesthetic truths. One's aesthetic
preferences and the details of what is appealing
about them have grown to be reliable and a part of
one's life, and it is this that is important.

With the right theoretical backing, it is
natural to think in a similar way about values and
morality. This is not to say that reason giving
becomes less important; indeed, one becomes better
at it. Nor is it to deny that moral reasons play a
different and more important role than do aesthetic
ones. The point I am making has rather to do with
the attitude one takes toward principles and their
application. When a person comes to know which of
his values are basic and which are secondary or
derivative, when he knows more facts, has had more
experience, and knows something about both the
frustration and success of moral argument, then he
is more likely to conclude he is not discovering
moral facts but responding to the nature of things.
An attitude that is sufficiently rooted in my nature
and in the facts, and which is not likely to be
overturned by the next trauma or news story, does
not require a moral fact to give it respectability.

Difficult problems lie ahead: Before we can
adequately discuss reasons, causes and rationality,

43

we must search out the boundaries of the moral. For not all opposition is moral opposition, not all favorable dispositions moral or normative ones. How can we elucidate the difference between moral and nonmoral opposition to something? This is the task of the next chapter.

Chapter II: NOTES

1   Richard Hare, FREEDOM AND REASON (New York,
     Oxford University Press, 1963), Chapter 2.

2.   THE RANDOM HOUSE DICTIONARY OF THE ENGLISH
     LANGUAGE (New York, 1966).

3.   John R. Searle, SPEECH ACTS: AN ESSAY IN THE
     PHILOSOPHY OF LANGUAGE (Cambridge: Cambridge
     University Press, 1969), pp 139-140.

4.   Searle, op. cit., p. 139.

5.   Ibid, p. 138.

6.   I owe this case to William Lycan.

7.   Richard Hare, op. cit., Chapter 4.

8.   Hume's TREATISE, Book III, Part I, Section I.

NORMATIVE BEHAVIOR

III. THE MARKS OF THE MORAL

3.1 <u>The Quest for the Generically Moral.</u> How are we to distinguish moral from nonmoral dispositions, "It's wrong" from "I don't like it"? It is perfectly possible to disapprove, command, or prescribe without making a moral judgment. Nondescriptivist analyses of moral sentences mask the problem because in analyzing only <u>moral</u> sentences, i.e., sentences using moral words such as "ought" and "right," they sidestep the question of why we say "It's wrong" instead of "I don't like it." They let the issue of whether we have a moral or nonmoral approval depend on whether a moral word is used, which leaves it a mystery why some pro and con dispositions get expressed with "oughts" and some do not. It is only because we already know how to distinguish moral from nonmoral approval that we know when to utter the "ought" sentence which the nondescriptivist then analyzes as, e.g., a prescription. This knowledge is part of our general linguistic competence; but that hardly releases philosophers from an obligation to explain the distinction. I like caviar and Art Nouveau, am averse to loud rock music and broken plumbing, but I do not claim these are matters of morals. Saying, "We manifest our opposition (or approval) with 'oughts' when our opposition is moral opposition" would be patently circular. Neither can we say "Our opposition is moral opposition when we express it in moral language," for this implies that it is impossible to misuse moral language and, more importantly, gives up attempting to explain why we use moral language about mugging people and not about broken plumbing.

Let me begin the attack on the problem of distinguishing moral from nonmoral disapproval in the light of Charles Stevenson's theory, which I think is as close to the truth as any. In ETHICS AND LANGUAGE, Stevenson's second pattern of analysis can be rephrased for "wrong" as follows:

'A is wrong' means 'A has qualities or
relations x,y,z,' except that 'wrong' has
as well an unfavorable emotive meaning
which permits it to express the speaker's
disapproval....[1]

A problem arises because Stevenson combines a
straightforward definition of a sentence with
explanatory remarks about a person's use or utterance of the sentence. The first half of his
analysis ("A has qualities or relations x,y,z") is a
partial definition of "A is wrong" and the second
half of it is a partial explanation of the speaker's
act of calling A wrong. But "A is wrong" and "Harry
says A is wrong" aren't the same thing; which of
them is supposed to get explained?

When Stevenson says that "wrong" has an
unfavorable emotive meaning which permits it to
express the speaker's disapproval, what is being
explained or analyzed here is not an action's being
wrong but some speaker using the word "wrong," in
other words, his calling something wrong. A
consequence of this is that Harry's expressing
disapproval of what ants do, when the ants do x,y,z,
is not even a putative counterexample to Stevenson's
analysis; for it is not a counterexample to an
analysis of "Harry says 'A is wrong'" unless Harry
happens to call what ants do wrong, and we can
suppose he does not.

A possible solution lies in bringing moral
beliefs as well as speech acts into the analysis. A
Stevensonian analysis of "Harry believes A is wrong"
might go as follows:

"Harry believes that A is morally wrong"
means "Harry believes that A has qualities
or relations x,y,z, and Harry is disposed
to express his disapproval of A."

With this definition of a moral belief the problem
that was sidestepped by analyses of moral sentences
comes to the surface, for now there are obvious
counterexamples: Harry's belief that playing loud
rock music is x,y,z, together with his disposition
to express disapproval of the music, would be a
moral belief. But it isn't. One might try an

alternative analysis:

> "Harry believes that A is wrong" means "Harry believes that A has qualities or relations x,y,z, and Harry is disposed to express his disapproval of A by calling A 'wrong'."

Definitions like these are too simple and too inflexible. I might be disposed to express disapproval by calling A wrong when I do not believe A is wrong, for example, if I misuse "wrong" and apply it to anything I dislike. Calling something morally wrong is not a sufficient condition for expressing a moral belief.

Neither is a person's calling something morally wrong (aloud or to himself) a necessary condition for expressing a moral belief. Harry might believe that A is wrong but not be disposed to call it wrong because he doesn't like the word "wrong." There are many people who refuse to use moral words, especially "wrong," "immoral," and "morally wrong." These people--often college students, soldiers, young blue collar workers--use the traditional moral terminology only to quote or for irony or mockery. They prefer profanity or expletives to express serious moral judgments: "Max is a bastard" or, "What Max did was shitty" (or "rotten," etc.). If they have fallen into the hands of social scientists their surrogate moral language may include such expressions as "dysfunctional" and "inappropriate."

Let us not despise these uses. They help us focus on the difference between moral and nonmoral opposition without allowing the traditional moral words, with all their associations and magic, to cloud the issue. The kinds of criteria I will suggest allow us to identify moral beliefs regardless whether or not someone uses moral words, which is as it should be. Suppose Harry says, "Max is a real bastard." Asked why, he replies that Max has spread malicious lies about Adolph and that is a rotten thing to do. Asked what is rotten about it, he either replies that it just is or he gets angry and shouts more invective. Has Harry taken a moral stand, or does he simply dislike what Max did? How does one tell? Is there something about what Harry

says, does, feels, or knows, which is lacking when
he calls Max a bastard because Max and he are rivals
for a woman or for a job, i.e., when he is not
morally opposed to Max's behavior? Whatever the
answer, we should be able to make the distinction
without having the magical words to lean on.

To this end we need to identify features which
are such that when enough of them are present people
are inclined to claim that we have a case of moral
opposition. These will not be "conceptual truths"
or "logical limits" on the "concept of morality." I
do not believe in such creatures. Nobody seems to
know what they mean, although this has not prevented
philosophers from using the jargon of logic and
epistemology to make rigorous sounding "points"
about "concepts." I shall offer empirical generalizations about behavior, verbal and nonverbal, which
hold often enough to be worth noting. Nonetheless,
when we are familiar with the generalizations and
with others like them, and with how deviations from
them strike us, and if they are correct, then we
will know roughly the boundaries of the notion of a
moral belief.

Self-interest is the main source of our nonmoral
opposition to things, people and their actions: If
someone believes his opposition is based only on
self-interest, he is not likely to believe he is
morally opposed nor is he likely to express himself
in moral language. Suppose that I oppose A
defeating B in competition for a job and admit it is
only because B is my friend. If I do not criticize
A's ability, methods, or character, it is almost
inconceivable that I would say that what A did was
immoral or unethical. I would hardly say, "A is
immoral because he won out over my friend." Suppose
instead that A robs B, spreads malicious lies about
him, or denies him money or privileges he grants to
others in B's situation. As in the previous case, I
have a self-interested reason for opposing what A
does because B is my friend. But if A's act is the
kind I would oppose even if it were done to a
stranger, then most likely I will claim I am morally
opposed and will use moral terminology in
manifesting my opposition.

Self-interested wants and aversions usually are expressed in the language of desire when they are about the actions of others: "I want him to do so-and-so." However, equally self-interested wants and aversions usually are expressed in normative language when they involve our own actions: "I shouldn't have bought it"; "I ought to apply for the job." The shift is significant and I wish to suggest an explanation. When I believe I ought to do something because it is in my interest, it is not at all problematic that the reason will appeal to the person to whom it is addressed, for that peron is myself. It is this difference that Kant had in mind when he distinguished between a "problematical" and an "assertorial" hypothetical imperative, the latter being an imperative or "ought" whose reason or basis is one's own happiness.[2] The explanation I suggest is that we tend to use normative language when the reason for our approval or opposition can be expected to appeal to those to whom it is addressed. By "those to whom it is addressed" I mean those persons in whose hands the feared or desired action lies. If, for reasons of self-interest, I oppose my doing X, I will say I shouldn't do X; if for the same reason I oppose your doing it, I will say I don't want you to do it. If the reason why I want other people to do X has no likelihood of appealing to them, then, even though X would benefit me, I am unlikely to use normative language. I say, "I don't want to lose my job" when the person who determines whether or not I keep it is someone else; I say "I ought not to quit my job" because the reason concerns the agent's self-interest. "I don't want to lose my job" as well as, "I ought not to quit my job" are nonmoral; in each case the reason for my opposition is self-interest. Nevertheless we use normative language in the one case but not in the other because the reason can be relied on to appeal to the agent in the one but not in the other.

The distinction also is relevant to morality. My moral reasons are expected to appeal to people in general with somewhat of the reliability with which my self-interested reasons are expected to appeal to myself. The wants and aversions behind my moral "shoulds" and "oughts" are ones I have at least some expectation will be shared by people other than myself and my friends. Even if my ought-judgment lacks a reason because it invokes an ultimate principle, I still expect that the want or opposition will be shared in my moral community. If I say I would like everyone to mail me a dollar because I want to be rich, I know that my reason is a self-interested one not likely to have a general appeal. I may say "I would like it if everyone were to mail the President a birthday card" (or if I am the boss, "Everyone will mail the President a nice birthday card"). The implication is that my reason, whether or not self-interested, is not likely to appeal to the people who would mail the birthday cards. However, if I say that everybody <u>should</u> mail me a dollar, or that everyone <u>should</u> mail the President a birthday card, the imp<u>lica</u>tion is that my reason will appeal to people other than myself and my friends. A belief is called moral partly because the reason has this kind of general appeal, not because it is, in itself, moral.

In our ancient, preliterate history moral language evolved to mark off what was required and forbidden in our tribe, as distinct from matters which were trivial or about which we bickered or went our own ways. It is perfectly natural that "oughts" and "ought nots" get applied to what <u>I</u> do for my own good, since my good (for me) and the tribal good (for us) equally were nonproblematic, fixed points. Minor courtesies aside, only children and childish or desperate adults offer self-interested reasons with the hope of winning agreement from people who have no special affection toward them. If we are not small children we know that the mere fact that I want something, together with the details of why I want it, is unlikely to be accepted by others as a reason for doing it. As I grow up I learn, painfully, that the "fixed point" my fellows accept is not my good but the common good. So I do not use "shoulds" and "oughts" to express self-interested wants except when the agent is myself. Moral "oughts" share with prudential "oughts" the feature of reliable appeal to the agent(s) addressed.

Self-interest is a clear and simple basis for distinguishing the moral from the nonmoral but, notoriously, only before philosophers get their hands on it. For this reason the likelihood of the reason's appealing to the potential agent is a better criterion. Self-interest is still a good clue to those desires and aversions which are unlikely to be shared. But if a philosopher expands the notion of self-interest to include our aversions to hurting or being unfair to strangers, which he can do because "self-interest" is vague, then it will not be a good clue to whether a want or aversion is a moral one, for the reason that it no longer tells us which of our reasons are likely to appeal to people besides ourselves and our friends.

3.2 <u>The Marks of the Moral.</u> Features that distinguish the moral from the nonmoral include the following. We are not inclined to morally judge something unless it is a person, or the action, state of character, moral opinion, or motive of a person. We seldom think an action morally right or wrong unless it benefits or harms people or the higher animals; or concerns human sexual behavior, patriotism, or the objects of religious prohibitions. We expect the reasons for a moral belief to appeal to the people who are being invited to accept it or act on it. We morally condemn reasonless inequalities in the distribution of benefits and penalties and in general insist that similar cases be judged similarly. We usually think of singular moral judgments as all-things-considered judgments and therefore as overriding ones. These generalizations are part of what enables us to predict when people will call opposition to something moral opposition and when they instead will consider it a mere dislike. But predicting word usage is secondary. I am not just interested in conditions which dispose a person to utter moral words, but in conditions that make a person's opposition moral opposition, whether or not he uses moral words. The use of moral language marks a real distinction, after all, else a peculiarly moral vocabulary would never have evolved. Just because of this I am also interested in words, for what people call a moral belief usually is a moral belief.

Old fashioned definists defined "right." New fashioned ones announced "conceptual limits" on the domain or function of morality. Now, presumably, we could deny that someone's belief is a moral belief even though he claims it is a moral belief, for example, if he says so-and-so is his moral opinion but is unwilling to universalize it. This was a great convenience: It gave us a way to refute our moral adversaries without morally disagreeing with them. However, neither the old nor the modern definism is satisfactory. If we define "right" in terms of some descriptive expression we not only imply that moral judgments are verifiable truths and falsehoods, we inevitably decide by definition controversial cases about what _is_ right. But if we define "moral belief" or the "institution of morality," beliefs which run afoul of the definition do not get classified as false moral beliefs, they get classified as nonmoral beliefs. What does the difference amount to? If we conclude on the basis of a definition that "Ants are immoral" does not express a moral belief, the person who seriously maintains that ants are immoral is rebutted as surely as he would if we had concluded on the basis of a definition that "Ants are immoral" is false. Suppose that we maintain, as a "conceptual point," that the aim of the institution of morality is to reconcile conflicts of interest, and suppose Freda maintains that conflict is good and social harmony is bad because it is a conspiracy to suppress the strong. We say, infuriatingly of course, "You are misusing moral language; therefore we don't need to get into moral argument with you." Nevertheless we have no compunction about saying that social disharmony and conflict are bad and evil; we are not ourselves misusing moral language in saying this.

This whole procedure appears to be no more than a trick. Definitions of "moral belief" or "the institution of morality" are persuasive definitions which decide questions of right and wrong as surely as do the less fashionable definitions of "right" and "wrong." They aim to allow us to refute the immoralist without getting into moral arguments with him; but the consequence is that he ceases to be an immoralist. Hence we cannot do what we want to do, namely condemn his moral beliefs as wrong moral beliefs, because they turn out not to be moral beliefs at all.

Is there any puzzle about the fact that my belief that eggs are 99¢ a dozen is not a moral belief whereas my belief that abortion is immoral is a moral belief? However, it does not help to be told that my belief that abortion is immoral is a moral belief. That is like being told that my belief that Webern's music is atonal is a musical belief. A person does not believe something is immoral just because he sincerely calls it so. On what basis, by what criteria, or under what conditions, does he call it so? An apparently obvious reply is, "He calls it immoral when he thinks it is immoral." Of course. But usually if he thinks it is immoral he says to himself that it is immoral, wrong, etc. And if he does not say to himself the characteristically moral words, on what basis, by what criteria, do we know that he <u>thinks</u> it is immoral? What is thinking something is immoral, in the absence of the magic words? On what basis does he either think or say to himself that it is immoral rather than, he dislikes it? "That depends on what his moral principles happen to be: ask him." And now we are asking for opinions and, it might seem, no longer asking what it is for a belief to be a moral one. I want to show, however, that what a moral belief is does depend on what people's moral opinions are.

There is one way we could give an extraterrestrial visitor a wholly adequate understanding of what moral words and sentences mean, though it is not a simple way: teach him our language. Newborn children are somewhat like extraterrestrial visitors and the method works with them. Meaning and opinion are inextricably bound together when children learn their native language. The examples of moral sentences that we imitate, respond to, and build out from are actual moral opinions of our parents and others around us. In this process what <u>sounds</u> allowable to say depends on how similar it is in syntax, subject matter, and context to actual moral opinions. Children acquire an ear for what sounds strange, silly, or unintelligible that only gradually grows to be relatively independent of opinion. The sense we have for what sounds strange, the capacity that often is called our linguistic intuition, seems indisputably to be a causal result of our linguistic experience.

"That is the man whom bought it" literally sounds wrong, quite apart from the fact that we can

formulate a rule that explains what is wrong with
it. The boundary between moral and nonmoral
beliefs, where both nonetheless concern norms, also
is marked by the sound different judgments have for
us. For example, I would teach my children that
saying "shit" or "fuck" is bad manners and vulgar;
but it would sound strange to claim that saying
those words is immoral or morally wrong. The
general distinction between manners and morals, and
the oddness of claims such as "Ants are immoral,"
can be formulated in rules, e.g., "Animals cannot be
moral or immoral." But whatever bite or authority
such a rule has derives from the fact that certain
kinds of utterances sound odd and are unshared.
They sound odd, ultimately, <u>because</u> they are
unshared.

This is a far cry from claims about a "logic" of
"moral discourse." How do philosophers justify the
move from the strange ring of a sentence to those
"conceptual points" which are employed to brand
moral sentences that offend against them as absurd,
misuses of language, conceptual errors, etc.? What
justifies the move from an empirical generalization
about how words and sentences <u>are</u> used to rules
framed in the jargon of logic or linguistics about
how words and sentences <u>must</u> or <u>cannot</u> be used? It
would be difficult to say precisely what principle
of logic a philosopher has in mind when he says
reasons of self-interest logically cannot be moral
reasons. What I think is true is that when someone
says self-interested reasons are not moral reasons,
he is stating popular moral opinion, but opinion so
stable and widespread that most deviations from it
cause the oddness reaction.

If we call the ant moralist's opinion a misuse
or a conceptual error, it is because it strikes no
chord in our feelings and interests and it deviates
too far from popular moral opinion. If a
philosopher claims that "Ants are immoral" is
excluded by the definition of "morality," he may
simply have invented a definition that excludes
sentences such as "Ants are immoral." If he does
invent a definition, it either conflicts with what
significant numbers of people believe and allow
themselves to say or it does not. If it does, then
the people who wish either to affirm or deny that

ants are immoral will simply reject it, and rightly so because it attempts to rebut their moral position with a stipulation. If it does not, then it gratuitously says that people "cannot" say what they already do not say.

One thing wrong with the notion of a conceptual error is that it does not admit of degrees. In reality, moral sentences slide imperceptibly from those most of us call wrong or incorrect to those we call silly, nonsensical or misuses of moral words. There is a change from quantity to quality when we jump suddenly from "taxation is immoral" to "aluminum is morally bad," but a continuum of intermediate cases lies between them. Moral sentences can get odder and odder and eventually reach a point at which we claim that Harry doesn't understand what "moral" and "immoral" mean; but that point is seldom reached. If most of the ant moralist's moral beliefs are as bizarre as his belief about ants, he doesn't use moral language in the way the rest of us do and hence he has, at best, an imperfect grasp of what moral language means and of what a moral belief is. Notice, however, that the charge we make is against him, not against some particular sentence he utters. Strictly speaking there is no such thing as the concept of the moral and making generalizations about uses of moral language is like sorting clouds. If a philosoper says that it is a logically necessary condition of a moral judgment that it be universalizable, he may know this because God whispers in his ear, but he certainly cannot deduce it from an examination of what people actually say and refrain from saying.

We appear to confront a mystery when we ask ourselves how or why, on some particular occasion, we know that the issue confronting us is a matter of morality and not a matter of simple dislike. For we do not go armed with criteria or a definition; we view the action and the words "wrong," "right," and their relatives just spring from our mouths or before our minds. It is understandable how philosophers should think that what cues us to say "wrong," "immoral" or "unethical" is an indefinable something which is wrongness itself or immorality itself or unethicalness itself. For must not the cue be what "wrong" means, either directly as the confrontation of what the word denotes, or by tracing reasons back to an ultimate one to which wrongess itself is stuck? It is not wrong to think that the meanings of words guide our use of them, for this may mean only that we have been successfully trained to the habit of using words as our linguistic community uses them. Believing that something is wrong is being opposed to it and hence disposed to do and say certain things. How we come to say or think moral words on particular occasions is no more mysterious than how we come to say or conclude that we like or dislike something. Likes and dislikes also are dispositions. If Harry especially likes turtles, or Art Nouveau, or a certain house, he usually but not always can give his reasons. But the "I like it" that he says aloud or to himself springs before his mind or from his mouth quite spontaneously, without any prior apprehension of a rule or scrutiny of reasons, as though he were suddenly confronted by likeableness itself.

Children learn quickly that what adults call wrong is behavior which is opposed and which prompts criticism; they learn that it is bad to kick one's sister, bad to make a mess or not pick up the toys, bad to be selfish and disregard the interests of others, and so on. At this stage it is not possible to distinguish between what young children believe is right and wrong and what they mean by "right" and "wrong." At first they agree with their parents' moral opinions, or more accurately, they say what their parents say, for it is unlikely that the moral sentences of the very young are backed by the appropriate dispositions. Perhaps this is the grain of truth in the cogitive-developmental theory of Lawrence Kohlberg, who maintains that children go through a fixed sequence of stages of moral development.[3] If learning moral ideas depends on ostensive teaching and, eventually, building out from learning-examples the child at first accepts as paradigms, Kohlberg's idea of a natural and pan-cultural development from a punishment/reward conception to (and hopefully through) a conventionalist conception of morality makes sense.

Almost at once children learn to deviate from their parents' opinions, while agreeing with what their parents mean. The key to how someone can morally disagree with his fellows and yet mean the same is a matter of not straying <u>too</u> far from the learning-examples and, later, from popular moral opinion; and it is also a matter of not straying too far from the kinds of feelings and dispositions other people have when they think something is wrong. We cling to two kinds of similarities with the great mass of past experience by which we were socialized and made members of a moral community. <u>First</u>, we stand by the kinds of dispositions and feelings that characterized our learning cases, e.g., we do not sincerely use "wrong" and similar words unless we are opposed or averse to the thing, nor do we use "right" unless we have some kind of favorable disposition. This is a necessary condition of knowing what a moral belief is and that is why it was made a matter of definition in Chapter Two.

<u>Second</u>, we cling to some of the actual features of the normative beliefs and judgments that comprised our socialization and upbringing. This second kind of guide functions as a control on the first, guaranteeing that we do not call just any opposition moral opposition or any approval moral approval. It is in this second condition that meaning and opinion meet, for it is not just general features of moral discourse such as the requirement that there be reasons, interpersonal appeal, or universalizability that guides us; it is also the actual nature of prevailing moral opinion such as the fact that morality concerns the behavior and well-being of people, not ants or celestial bodies.

So the marks of the moral are both substantive and formal. Once having internalized them we can identify moral beliefs in a way that is detachable from standard moral terminology: Moral beliefs are favorable or unfavorable dispositions that bear enough of the marks of the moral. On this view a moral belief is a real thing, adequately describable without the use of terms like "moral belief," and therefore people who abandon moral language or children whose parents are progressive types who never taught them moral language, are not necessarily moral nihilists. People like A. S. Neill of SUMMERHILL notoriety,[4] together with the American moral education faddists of the 1960's and 1970's, were just bursting with moral beliefs and principles

with which they indoctrinated school children; but
they would be aghast at the idea and they never let
an "ought" or a "thou shalt not" fall from their
lips.

We do not consciously learn the differentia of
moral opposition. We are exposed to them and a
causal result of this exposure is our ear for the
difference between ethics and mere wants and hates.
There is nothing peculiar about the opposition
itself; qua opposition, moral opposition is perfectly ordinary opposition. But it tends to get manifested by the use of moral words when it bears the
marks of the moral. Moral language is simply the
language we are taught to use when we either talk
about or manifest dispositions with certain
empirical features. The claim that "right" or
"wrong" is the correct word to use is neither
normative nor epistemic, it is taxonomic.

Facts about human nature, the requirements of
social living, and our environment, cause moral
beliefs to be the kind of things they are, with the
general identifying features I call the marks of the
moral. Asking how it might have been otherwise is
speculating about the consequences if we were
biologically different kinds of creatures; it is
like asking what our morality might have been if
people were radially rather than bilaterally symmetrical, or were immortal, or reproduced asexually,
or had larval, pupal and imago stages like butter-
flies. Even in these fanciful circumstances, if the
beings were rational, social, and had wants, we
would expect them to have serious oppositions some
of which were backed by reasons that had a general
appeal; we would expect them to universalize and
have overriding opposition to what threatened their
group; this group would be their moral community,
within which they would expect their reasons to have
an appeal. The oppositions and approvals that had
these features would be their morality.

The use of moral language is one of the marks of
the moral and therefore prima facie evidence for a
moral belief. In certain contexts, if someone
sincerely says he believes so-and-so is immoral,
then he does believe it is immoral. If someone says
he is an ethical egoist most of us are inclined to

60

concede that he is one, that is, we are inclined to admit that there can be moral beliefs based entirely on self-interest. Important features of ethics are absent from ethical egoism and we would never think of calling egoists' beliefs moral ones if they used the language of desire and aversion (but otherwise thought, spoke and acted like the egoist who did use moral language). Ethical egoism plainly has some of the marks of the moral: the egoist's normative judgments are about people and the actions of people, they concern good and harm that are done, and his "shoulds" and "oughts" are overriding ones. So in this kind of mixed case normative judgments and beliefs based on self-interest are moral ones if a person calls them so.

It especially pays to attend to the oppositions and approvals of people who get along without moral language, while adapting other words to do the old jobs. If their reasons are universalizable, all-things-considered ones that have general appeal and concern human welfare, etc., then nothing is lost but a word. If everybody were to express and talk about their approvals and oppositions in the language of desire and aversion, or in the language of profanity, the taxonomic features that count would not disappear, and in one respect we would be better off: All of the chatter about moral properties and sui generis moral feelings or perceptions would cease. Not in their most soaring hypostatic moods would it occur to philosophers to claim, when Harry says "What Max did was really shitty," that Harry was attributing a simple non-natural property or relation called "shittiness" to Max's action; or if Harry says that he is very much opposed to abortion and gives universalizable reasons, that Harry was attributing a property to abortion in addition to those he names when he gives his reasons.

People who refrain from using moral language doubtless do so for reasons other than to combat bad moral metaphysics. They fear that the use of traditional moral language will brand them with traditional moral opinions; they may think of morality as primarily a matter of indoctrination and moralistic hectoring; and finally, they may think that the "emotive force" of the traditional language is worn out and no longer appropriate to their feelings.

On the other hand the language of morality is much exploited and abused in order to dignify perfectly ordinary hatreds, dislikes and aversions. People can get away with this if they do not stray too far from the central core of what traditionally are counted as moral issues. A sexual prude maintains that even mildly prurient movies are immoral; a utopian capitalist says that levying an income tax is morally wrong, a utopian socialist that buying stocks is wicked; a patriot finds morally intolerable the most minor breach of protocol regarding the care of his country's flag; and various gentle souls proclaim it to be immoral to shoot rats or pigeons. These people do not <u>have</u> to call these things immoral. I do not mean <u>that</u> their opposition is not sincere. But I think that sometimes they themselves feel, in the privacy of their own minds, that they are stretching things a bit in making a moral issue of the matter. The issues are of such a nature, their reasons and feelings of such a kind, that if they expressed their views without moral language, it would be most natural to understand them as personal or political ideals, as wants, or simple squeemishness.

In this shadow area their calling something a matter of morality can make it so, and in so doing they may commit themselves to a pattern of behavior appropriate to moral opposition: they are now prepared to "stand on principle," make serious speeches, and refuse to compromise; and all because the words "It's <u>immoral</u>" tumbled from their mouths in their fervor to give their opposition some weight. The difference between moral and nonmoral opposition can be as slight as this. Nonetheless, sometimes people have extremely poor grounds for using moral language and it is obvious they merely want strong words to give greater weight to their hatreds and dislikes. And sometimes people lie: They express what they know to be their ordinary likes and dislikes as though they were moral beliefs.

Chapter III: NOTES

1. Charles L. Stevenson, ETHICS AND LANGUAGE (New Haven; Yale University Press, 1944), p. 207.

2. Kant, FUNDAMENTAL PRINCIPLES OF THE METAPHYSICS OF MORALS, Second section.

3. Lawrence Kohlberg, "Stage and Sequence: The Cognitive-Developmental Approach to Socialization," in David A. Goslin (ed.), HANDBOOK OF SOCIALIZATION THEORY AND RESEARCH (Chicago: Rand McNally College Publishing Co., 1969).

4. A. S. Neill, SUMMERHILL: A RADICAL APPROACH TO CHILD REARING (New York: Hart Publishing Co., 1960). The most influencial American moral education book of the pseudo-nondirective school was VALUES AND TEACHING, by Louis E. Raths, Merrill Harmin, and Sidney B. Simon (Columbus, Ohio: Charles Merrill Co., 1978).

IV. UNIVERSALIZABILITY AND THE SELF

4.1 Universal Rules and Particular Persons. In the preceding two chapters I outlined some elements of a dispositional/emotivist ethical theory. Now I return to topics touched on in Chapter One concerning the relation of the self to morality and to society. Our story is a classic one of universals and particulars, and how they can possibly coexist, only here the one protagonist is the impartial self of repeatable features and the other is our awareness of the particularity of the self. I begin with an effort at formulating a satisfactory version of the principle that genuine moral judgments are univeralizable ones. Consider:

> (S) Two things cannot differ only as regards goodness.

This is called the "supervenience" principle by Richard Hare and, decades earlier, referred to as the "consequential" or "resultant" character of moral judgments by G. E. Moore and David Ross. An equivalent statement of it is that if two things are nonmorally similar they must be morally similar. (S) is a strong claim and it entails the version of universalizability that is important for ethics, the simplest form of which is,

> (U1) If A is good, then anything similar in all nonmoral respects is also good.

(U1) merely reformulates (S). It is not very useful since one isn't likely to encounter two things that are similar in all their nonmoral respects.

> (U2) If A is good, then anything exactly similar is also good.

This is a trivial tautology if being good counts as a similarity. If we stipulate that only properties of A and B count as similarities, then whether (U2) is trivially true depends on whether "good" names a

65

property: If both have goodness, both are good. If "good" is not the name of a property, (U2) is equivalent to (U1), in which case it, too, is entailed by (S). And what (S) says is that there are reasons for moral and evaluative differences between things, these reasons being other differences between those things. This claim is certainly not a trivial tautology. Indeed, we shall see that there is at least one way to differently evaluate two things that have all the same properties.

(S) entails (U2), because if nonmoral similarity implies moral similarity, a fortiori exact similarity also implies moral similarity. But (U2) does not entail (S), because things can be nonmorally similar without being exactly similar: (U2) would be trivially true and (S) false if having the unique moral property "goodness" were the only similarity relevant to being good. For these reasons (U2) is not of much use.

> (U3) If A is good, then anything similar in all morally relevant respects is also good.

There is, unfortunately, a conceivable situation in which (U3) is true and (S) false, this again being the situation in which the unique moral property goodness is the only feature relevant to being good. This is sufficient to ruin (U3) as a useful generalization principle.

> (U4) If A is good, then anything similar in all nonmoral, morally relevant respects is also good.

This is the full-fledged universalizability principle in ethics. (U4) makes it explicit that there are nonmoral reasons for moral differences between things. If we understand (S) to presuppose that nonmoral differences are "relevant," then (S) and (U4) are equivalent. Given this, all one really requires for a universalizability principle in ethics is (S), the supervenience principle.

If universalizability is taken to be a requirement of a genuine moral judgment, there is a feature of it that constitutes a serious difficulty for ethical intuitionism. Contrast a pair of yellow chairs with a pair of good chairs: Someone might admit that two chairs cannot differ only in color (on the ground there must be other, chemical differences that cause the color difference), but nevertheless maintain that yellow was the only difference between them that he happened to notice. This can't happen in the moral case: It sounds incoherent to say that while he knows the two chairs cannot differ only as regards goodness, nevertheless the only difference he happens to notice is that one of them is a good chair and the other is not. It is one thing to say that there must be reasons, i.e., nonmoral differences, that account for a value or moral difference between two things; it is another thing to say that people must have reasons when they judge things to differ morally or evaluatively. The first of these claims does not imply the second. Supervenience and universalizability are usually explained as saying that there must be reasons for the goodness or rightness of things. But that makes those principles too weak; they should be interpreted as saying that people must have reasons.

Sometimes people say they do not know why they think one picture is better than another (although this seldom is said about persons), but I suggest that what is meant is that they do not know which, among various observed differences, are the ones in virtue of which they think one is better than the other. It would be weird, almost frightening, if someone said he saw no difference besides the value difference: What if he could always tell you which was the good one of several perfect prints from the same plate, tracking it by its goodness even when you shuffled them behind his back? The strangeness would not be mitigated if he went on to say that, while he admits there must be another difference because evaluative judgments are supervenient, nonetheless and as it happens, he noticed only the value difference.

Intuitionists such as G. E. Moore and David Ross, who based universalizability (in the sense of U4) on synthetic necessary connections between moral and nonmoral properties, must deny the difference I have been describing: They must say that the moral case is like the color case. Even if the intuitionists established that moral principles are synthetic necessary truths, they are still trapped: They must concede that they could intelligibly affirm that A was good and B was not good, concede that therefore A and B must differ in some additional respect, and nevertheless go on to affirm that goodness was the only difference between A and B they happen to notice. If goodness were a distinct property it would be possible to apprehend an unconnected goodness, whatever its quasi-logical connections with other properties, and hence possible that it be the only apprehended difference between two things. Someone may, for example, just be incompetent at discerning synthetic necessary connections. For properties are what one can just apprehend, like yellow or sweetness, whether or not there also are reasons (or causes) why they are present. Given that goodness is a property at all, only if it were identical with some other property, as the naturalists claim, would it be impossible or unintelligible to notice only a normative difference between two things. If the connection between goodness and nonmoral property X is contingent or synthetic necessary, goodness and X are two properties, each in principle discernible by itself.

Let us now divide normative beliefs and judgments into two classes: universalizable, impersonal ones and self-dependent ones. Self-dependent norms depend on viewing things as in some sense one's own. My belief that I should do X is self-dependent if it is essential that it involves me or mine: my happiness, my children, my community, my feelings, my country, my species, residents of my galaxy, etc. The mark of a self-dependent judgment is my unwillingness to eliminate self-referential words such as "I" or "mine." By contrast, impersonal morality essentially refers only to repeatable features of things such as "pleasant," "expensive," "black," "white," etc. The distinction between self-dependent and impersonal normative beliefs is the important distinction between kinds of normative beliefs and it is essential to understanding the nature of egoism, loyalties, and social morality. Let us first see how self-dependent norms--egoism and group loyalties--differ from impersonal ones.

Compare "I ought to protect the blond child first" with "I ought to protect my child first." If someone claims that he ought to protect child C because the child is blond, he judges in terms of an ideal or value, and he is committed, unless he finds other reasons, to protecting any child that is blond. So too, if he judges that he ought to attend to a small child about to do something dangerous, consistency requires a similar judgment in similar circumstances. If he judges that he ought to protect child C because the child is his child, the situation is radically different, since "his child" does not name any repeatable feature in addition to that of being a child. If this is the reason (and if it counts as a reason at all), it is, in one important respect, a non-universalizable reason: He can without inconsistency deny that he has a similar obligation to Freda's exactly similar child, which he would not be able to do if he had based his judgment on some repeatable feature that was shared by his child and Freda's child. For the basis of his judgment is that the child is his, not that it has a certain feature. I do universalize "I ought to save my child first" up to a point: If I have more than one child I must admit I ought to save each of them ahead of other people's children, since each is a similar case in virtue of being a child of mine.

Let us at once clear away some possible confusions about universalizing. There are at least three ways to universalize "H ought to protect his own child":

(1) H ought to protect any similar child.
(2) Everybody similar to H ought to protect H's child.
(3) Everybody ought to protect his own child.

H might think consistency requires accepting (3); but, if his reason is that the child is his child, consistency does not require that he accept (1). Because his reason is simply that the child is his, and not that it has some protection-warranting feature $\emptyset$, his normative judgment need not be universalized in way (1). He may go on to claim that everyone has a similar non-universalizable obligation to protect his or her own child ahead of other people's children.

The case is exactly analogous to the more familiar one of egoism. An egoist says, "I ought to look out for myself first," and he might feel required to be a universal egoist and also say, "Everybody ought to look out for himself first." But if he is an egoist at all, his reason for thinking he should perform some act is simply that it benefits himself, which is a reason that is not universalizable in way (1). For, however similar another person may be to him, his reason will not oblige him to benefit that other person, because it is not a question of similarities. The logic of "I should do it because it benefits my so-and-so" and "I should do it because it benefits me" is the same.

"My" does not name a repeatable feature or define a class, neither does "her." So there is no morally decisive feature that applies to my children and not Freda's: What I take to be relevant about my children is not that they are children, nor that they are some person's children, but that they are mine. Nor is it relevant that Freda's judgment can have the same form of words as mine, i.e., "I ought to save my child first." "I" said by Freda does not refer to the same thing as "I" said by me, though it might refer to an exactly similar kind of thing.

Normative judgments based on egoism and normative judgments based on loyalties share the characteristic of containing uneliminable egocentric particulars. If I say that I ought to defend my country, I have a putative loyalty. But if I am willing to replace "my country" with, e.g., "a democratic country" or "a Christian country," I don't have a loyalty but an ideal; in this case what I am committed to is a kind of thing, not some particular thing. If I am unwilling to replace "my country" with a characterizing expression, I have a genuine loyalty and not an ideal; my normative judgment is self-dependent.

If I have a reason that is a repeatable feature of A, I must universalize; on the other hand, if I have in mind no relevant difference at all between A and B, I must judge A and B similarly. Between the two it may be tempting to think that a relevant difference must be a repeatable feature. Nonetheless, I can find A and B relevantly different without the difference being a matter of repeatable features: The difference can be that A is mine and B is not. I may not appeal to features, but that fact will not erase what the whole world knows to be a most obvious and important difference, namely the difference every person expresses when he distinguishes between "mine" and "thine." There is all the difference in the world, for me, between my happiness and your happiness or, when they are different, between my country and yours or my species and yours. Hence, self-dependent judgments that a person refuses to universalize are not arbitrary. Neither are they inconsistent, for I do not value my happiness or my country on the basis of a property that also belongs to your happiness or your country. I certainly do not value these things because they belong to "the agent" or "the speaker"; I value them because they belong to me.

This brings out an important difference between egocentric particular terms and other kinds of singular terms. If I say that Harry is a good man and Max is not, or that America ought to be defended by its citizens and the USSR not, I am being arbitrary and irrational if I have no reason. "America," used as a pure label, does not name a difference between America and the USSR. It is not merely that it does not pick out a property or relation; it does not pick out any difference. Patriots, if they wish to avoid the requirement to universalize their patriotic judgments, must say that they ought to defend America because it is their country, and not because it is America. But more on patriotism later.

Can "It is my child" count as a moral reason? We might say No, on the ground that I merely repeat myself when I answer the question "Why do you think you should save your child first?" with "Because she is mine." But note the equally repetitive, "Why is it good just because it is pleasant?"--"Because pleasure is good." So perhaps there are certain particulars as well as kinds that we can value without being able to say why we value them. I may not have any reason why pleasure is good and pain is bad; nevertheless when I make such judgments I cannot be convicted of judging similar cases dissimilarly, for pleasure is no more pain than is my child Freda's child.

There are a variety of self dependent norms, for example, obligations based on love. People we love are particulars that are distinguished from similar things by their relation to another particular, namely oneself. If a man loves a woman, a father loves his daughter, or a person loves his country, and he is threatened with its loss, it will not do to tell him not to worry because we will get him another one just as good. It is _that_ _one_ that he loves and "that one" is not a characterizing expression. It is irrelevant that the lover could, in principle, be fooled by a substitute, or that he will accept substitutes with the passage of time. Of course, this kind of love does not always give rise to a sense of obligation, but when it does, it is self-dependent obligation.

Loyalty is another disposition whose object is a particular thing and not a kind of thing. If Harry is loyal to his friend George, he sticks by this person and not by just any person who has such and such characteristics. A person doesn't love or have loyalty to something because it is a thing of a certain kind, such that he would equally love or be loyal to what he knew was a similar, substituted thing; he loves or is loyal to _that thing_. Loyalty and that highly visible form of it called patriotism are said to be irrational precisely because they have these features.

4.2 _Tribal Morality._ One temptation is to think that any genuine morality must be wholly impersonal and based only on repeatable features. This seems plausible when we focus on the competition of morality and egoism. But other self-dependent moral beliefs concern joint possessions such as a profession, a community, a country, or a species, regarding which a great many people can say "mine." These beliefs satisfy the condition, which egoism does not, of having a general appeal within a community, and thereby possess one of the marks of the moral.

It is not inappropriate to call self-dependent morality of this kind "group egoism." But it is not egoistic in the sense of selfish, since loyalty to family, community or country transcends the self and can demand a complete sacrifice of what ordinarily is called self-interest. Self-dependent morality is the morality of loyalties, loves, and possessions, but of shared as well as unshared ones. It is tribal morality. Mankind is a tribe and philosophers whose moral good is based on the peace and happiness of Mankind rather than on some set of features which, as luck would have it, humans just happens to possess, have a self-dependent, tribal morality. Utilitarians maintain that the highest good is the greatest happiness of the greatest number of people. Why people rather than turtles or lions? Perhaps only people are capable of happiness. Then why happiness unless it is because it is what people desire and can attain? Mankind happened to be John Stuart Mill's species. We can better understand his principle if we say, "the highest good is the greatest happiness of the greatest number of _my_ species." To be sure, his parochialism is broader than that based on "my fellow citizens," "my family," or "my bodily pleasures." But when it is expressed as a self-dependent principle it is as exempt from generalizations to similar species as egoism is exempt from generalization to similar persons.

Some of our loyalties are wide, some are narrow, and they are nested and overlapping. I may be loyal to my community and also to my country, a wider domain that includes my community, and again to my species, a still wider domain. When we represent a person's system of loyalties by ellipses and concentric circles, we can let the center point be the self, the "inward" logical limit on self-dependent morality. The ever larger circles represent ever wider loyalties. Is there an "outer" limit as well as an "inward" one, such as one's species or the members of one's galaxy? I shall defend the position that there is no outer limit to our loyalties that rational thinking can discover, although there are psychological limits.

When a person's nested loyalties clash we face the problem of the relative authority of parts and

wholes. Is it better or more rational to support my
city to the disadvantage of my neighborhood, or to
support my neighborhood to the disadvantage of my
city? Am I a traitor to my neighborhood if I yield
to the claims of some larger whole? In the

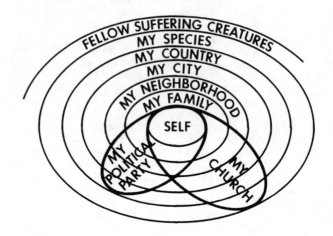

Figure One:
GROUP EGOISM AND THE ETHICS OF PARTS AND WHOLES

Our nested and overlapping group loyalties
define domains of social morality, moral
communities within which we universalize and
treat similar cases similarly. Egoists make
the inmost point their supreme value, their
moral energy diminishing as they move out from
the center. Utilitarians make the widest
circle supreme, thinking it corresponds with
humanity; their motto is, "more is better." If
we define a fanatic as someone who fixates on
one of these circles and says it always comes
first, whatever the consequences for other
people's lives or ideals, both egoists and
utilitarians will be fanatics.

political arena it is commonly argued that the
conflict is unreal, the city saying that what is
good for the whole is good for the part and the
neighborhood saying that what is good for the part

74

is good for the whole. Each argues that the rational interests of both parties are served by its position because any other defense implies that someone must be sacrificed, which produces an irresolvable adversarial situation. These arguments are very often sophistical; it often is simply false that what is good for the whole is good for the part. What is good for Columbus may not be good for a neighborhood, what is good for America may not be good for Columbus or for General Motors, and what is good for the world may not be good for America. So too, going the other way.

Though it cannot reasonably be denied that the good of the whole often is incompatible with the good of a part or constitutive unit, utilitarians would argue that our duty is to Humanity and that doing what benefits your neighborhood or country is wrong if it prevents a greater good for a larger whole. On this view, the wider the loyalty, the greater the moral claim it usually has on us, and regional competition for resources or benefits is justified only when it is the more efficient way to maximize the good of everyone. The utilitarian position seems to present a dilemma for those who wish to take loyalties seriously. Should university administrators, community leaders, mayors, or presidents always adopt the impartial point of view regarding the allocation of goods? They often will be disloyal to their constituencies if they do, and they will be judged unethical, from the point of view of the "general good," if they do not. The utilitarian asks, rhetorically, "Does the mere fact that a university, community, or nation is yours add, even in the slightest degree, to the case for its deserving a benefit or advantage?"

There are two reasons why the utilitarian attack on loyalties is unconvincing. The first is that utilitarianism itself simply assumes that species loyalty is always the most demanding one. If it is claimed that it is the most demanding loyalty because it is the widest, this in turn implying that the most good and harm are at stake, the claim is incorrect. Wider conceptions of one's own kind can be in terms of rational beings, beings capable of suffering, living beings, and so on. If family loyalty and patriotism are biases, in the sense of favoring a particular group because it is one's own, so too is the claim that the good is the happiness of human beings. The argument is this: If the elimination of human suffering is more important than the elimination of animal suffering, the ground is either a reasonless bias in favor of one's own species or some list of features that warrants protecting beings with those features. But any list is bound to fail always to protect humans, because of what we might call "the problem of imperfect specimens." No matter what the list, some human cases of senility or mental defect will satisfy it less well than some gorillas or chimpanzees, and so we would be forced to justify using the human ahead of the chimp for medical experiments; such a position would not be a utilitarian one. Of course, someone might abandon the search for "relevant" features and just list the taxonomic differentia of humans; in that case we would be justified in saying the list was just a rationalization for species bias. The utilitarian cannot make his case by criticizing community loyalists or patriots for being in a similar position.

Second, it is not obvious that wider loyalties always take moral precedence over narrower ones. We are often told to look beyond our neighborhood, city, or country in the name of impartiality, and treat what we had hitherto favored as our own as just one among many neighborhoods, cities, or countries. But the demand for impartiality is never true impartiality, it is merely an invitation to give one's loyalty to a larger whole with which someone identifies; in other words, an invitation to join a larger tribe. If our first love is to some narrower group this forced shift may render our moral concern weak and pallid. Equal moral concern for the whole of humanity or the whole of sentient nature is, for most of us, too diluted to generate effective moral enthusiasm and too weak to outweigh narrower loyalties.

If one thinks that the wider loyalty _must_ carry greater moral weight because it is wider, it is important to remember that it identifies one's kind under a different description than the narrower loyalty. The nature of the description as well as the size of the domain it defines determine how much

I care about my kind under that description. This consideration by itself refutes the utilitarian claim that more is always better. I have extremely weak galaxy-member loyalty relative to species loyalty, and weak species loyalty relative to family loyalty. More is not always better because it is not always more of the same thing. Hence, without further argument it will not do to claim, in the name of speciesism, that nationalism, community loyalty, and family loyalty count for less because they count for fewer.

What this implies is the defensibility of the position that sometimes what benefits my family obligates me more than does a greater benefit to the whole of humanity; and also that a still greater benefit (or threat) to humanity might nevertheless obligate me on the side of humanity. It implies the acceptance of a world in which rational, moral people can have loyalties that are in limited competition with those of other people, for example, members of different families, communities, or nations. If this is so, the rational community leader is not always obliged to be a traitor: he need not accept the expressway that obliterates his neighborhood just because he sees it is likely to produce a small, offsetting greater good for some larger whole. If he is intellectually honest with himself he admits that his own neighborhood counts more for him than do other people's neighborhoods. This is the equivalent in microcosm of the patriot who says his own country counts more for him than do other people's countries, and the person who says that his own species counts more for him than other species. There is no implication of, "My community, right or wrong" or "My country, right or wrong," because group loyalties determine obligations only prima facie: This is an implication of most people's understanding of the ethics of parts and wholes. Even if someone admits that, say, family loyalty is his strongest loyalty, it should not be forgotten that the good and harm at stake comes in degrees. Such a person has no reason to deny that a small family sacrifice still can be outweighed when it is balanced against some significant harm to be avoided (or good to be achieved) by his community or his country.

Should we conclude that group loyalty is just a bias, that it is the enemy of morality, and be done with it? Think of what tribalism in the form of racism and nationalism have brought upon the world. Before I take up the general question, in terms of a suggestion I wish to develop about the relation between loyalties and impersonal morality, it should be noted that racism usually depends on ignorance of the nature of race differences and on hostile, false claims about other races. Family, community, and civic loyalties seldom have those features. A loyalty, like any norm, can be rationally faulted if it depends on ignorance of facts. It is not even obvious that racism is a loyalty, logically on all fours with patriotism or community loyalty. This is because racism is negative, being much more concerned with hatred of other races than with pride in one's own, whereas loyalty is positive and is primarily characterized by esteem and concern for the common good of one's group.

4.3 <u>Patriotism.</u> It is fashionable in some circles to view patriotism with contempt, as disreputable as racism. For why, it is asked, ought I give any greater support to my country over another, in a controversy between them, merely because one of them is my country? Should I not support whichever country a disinterested, rational, informed observer would support? Yet, loyalty to one's family, community, or species is seldom treated with the contempt with which patriotism is treated. They are equally biases. Then should loyalties never enter into our deliberations about what we should do? It is possible that without loyalties there would be no values or morality at all, and that even appeals to rationality and the capacity to suffer are commitments to the protection of one's kind under a certain description. Even so, is there something special about patriotism? Is it, perhaps, a defective kind of group loyalty?

I wish to distinguish three types of patriotism: impartial patriotism, sports patriotism, and loyalty patriotism. As we shall see, impartial patriotism arises from the demands of wider loyalties, sports patriotism arises from pressure to universalize patriotic judgments. A case can be made that only loyalty patriotism should be called patriotism.

Loyalties are norms that define the domains within which we accept the moral machinery of impartial judging and relevant differences. This machinery makes moral argument, hence the possibility of persuasion, possible; the naked declaration of a loyalty makes it impossible. Consequently whatever kind of patriot we are, we have every reason to try to find a basis for dialogue with the competitor, the Spartan, or the Andromedan, for it supplements the possibility of winning by force or trickery with the possibility of winning (or cutting losses) by reasoning and persuasion. But it also adds the possibility of being obliged to lose. This is a way of saying that it is to my advantage that the beings I must confront be members of one of my moral communities, for that means we share a noninstrumental good, which in turn opens the possibility of persuading them not to eat me or enslave me.

An impartial patriot is someone who maintains that only such considerations count. In defending his country's policy in a war or international confrontation he appeals only to truly international principles of political morality, for example, that his country is democratic, or is on the side of "the people," or was intolerably provoked. His position is that he ought to support whichever country has features A...N; and, as luck would have it, that happens to be his own country. Impartial patriotism is not loyalty in the sense defined in Section 4.1 because the reasons such "patriots" give do not contain uneliminable self referential terms. An impartial patriot says he supports his country just because it has certain features, therefore implying that if his country and its adversary exchanged these features he should support the adversary. If it is true that he supports his country solely because he thinks it is in the right, it follows that its being his does not enter at all into his decision. Such "patriots" believe themselves to be objective, like ideal observers, and simply lucky their country is right, whereas I think most of us believe their underlying motives are pure loyalty and their reasons rationalizations. Americans who supported North Vietnam and the Viet Cong during the war indeed did take the "impartial point of view" (unless they simply had a different loyalty), and some called themselves true patriots for doing so.

Perhaps we should recognize a second type of impartial patriot, namely anyone who actually convinces himself that his country is always the best, which rules out having to support adversaries. I think, however, that we are willing to acknowledge either type as patriotism only because we believe the reasons impartial patriots give are rationalizations: we call impartial patriots "patriots" because we think that, deep down, they are loyalty patriots and not because we think impartial patriotism, in itself, is patriotism.

By contrast a loyalty patriot concedes that what he should do is partly determined by the fact that the good of his country is at stake. But he need not affirm that it is wholly determined by this. He thinks the fact that P is his country can outweigh some (but not necessarily all) reasons of the sort a distinterested international observer would consider. That a party to the dispute is his own country is a relevant consideration in his thinking about which country he should support. To a loyalist, the thought, "P is my country," though it counts for something, need not outweigh moral arguments against reprisal or military intervention, whereas to an impartial patriot the thought, "P is my country," is not conceded to count for anything. A distinction should be noted between what a patriot thinks he is personally obliged to do and what he thinks his country should do. Many patriotic normative judgments can be expressed only by public affirmation or the ballot, unless a citizen happens to be President or Secretary of State. A patriot may say, "America ought to take reprisal if hostages held in a foreign country are killed," although this is not something he personally can do, nor even something he necessarily should assist, since assistance (in military service or otherwise) depends on personal circumstances; for example, a pregnant woman with other children to care for may have no personal obligation in the matter.

It might be thought that patriotism can be based on a universalizable obligation a citizen has and a disinterested international observer lacks: an obligation of gratitude for the education, protection, and freedoms a country provides its citizens. First, this makes loyalty a matter of owed payment, and explains patriotism in terms of a commercial relation between an individiual and society. Gratitude presupposes a debt, loyalty presupposes a prized or loved object and a sense of possession. Second, although gratitude might partly justify ceremonial patriotism such as celebrations and flag-tending, I doubt that gratitude can ever override moral reasons. Suppose George and Harry are rivals in the heroin trade, and I owe George a debt of gratitude. If I help George kill Harry, the wrongness of my act is not diminished in the slightest by the fact that I owe gratitude to George. What I owe George out of fairness or because of a contract can compete with other moral considerations; but what I owe him out of gratitude does not compete at all with contrary moral considerations. So too, it appears, if America is in conflict with P, whatever moral reasons there are against supporting the American cause are not countered by any amount of gratitude owed to America. But this assumes we always can sharply distinguish gratitude from loyalty. Certainly, the services for which one owes gratitude, such as education and protection, can also be causes of loyalty.

The patriot's dilemma is that he seems forced to choose between the death of loyalty and mindless confrontations of pure tribalism. On the one hand, patriotism is a mere bigotry if it is true that national interests ought to be completely subordinated to impartial adjudication in terms of more general principles. The impartial patriot grasps this horn of the dilemma, but still chooses to call himself a patriot. On the other hand, a patriot who says he should help P defeat Q because P is his country seems required to admit that Q's patriots have a corresponding duty to help defeat P. That is, he seems required to maintain that this is what they really ought to do, not just that it is what they think they ought to do. The question of what other nations' patriots ought to do arises as surely as the egoist's familiar problem regarding what he thinks other egoists ought to do. If an egoist is either formally or pragmatically inconsistent when he universalizes, as when an egoist in a lifeboat with another egoist says each ought to throw the

other to the sharks, a patriot who says competing
foreign patriots have obligations like his own will
be inconsistent for the same reason.

The sports patriot grasps this horn of the
dilemma and attempts to cope with universalized
patriotic obligations by modeling them after
loyalties to sports teams. Suppose a loyal fan of
the Ohio State football team is asked by a
philosopher, "But which team ought to win?" The fan
is loathe to claim either that his team ought to win
just beause it is his, or that he should abandon his
loyalty and support the team that most deserves to
win in the light of impartial critiera. He
therefore says that each team ought to try to win
and, if pressed about which of them ought to
succeed, says the "best" team should win. A patriot
who takes this line claims that each nation's
citizens ought to try to further their respective
national interests and, in the case of war, try to
defeat the other. In doing so the sports patriot,
like the impartial patriot, masks his loyalty by
affirming more universal values which have nothing
to do with national loyalty. His values are "trying"
and, ultimately, such qualities as toughness and
competence. He is worse off than the impartial
patriot, who at least rationalizes that his country
is the best. Committed to universalizing, the
sports patriot claims that when it comes to war Q
ought to try to do in his country and his ought to
try to do in Q; but he cannot explain why someone
who calls himself a patriot should affirm both of
these propositions.

This leaves us with loyalty patriotism. How is
it to be defended? Let us briefly consider family
loyalty, about which American intellectuals are less
nervous and ambivalent than they are about
patriotism, and I shall assume that whatever we can
conclude about the one case we can conclude in
principle about the other. For I wish to defend the
idea of loyalty patriotism, not some particular
instance of it. A felt obligation to assist one's
family is a case of taking care of one's own. Yet
the obligation is not just self-interested or
prudential. The judgments we are inclined to make
about someone who is unwilling to save his own child
first are very unlike our response to imprudence.

82

Suppose we witness the following scene. A family is vacationing at the beach; as the father walks up on the pier he sees his daughter and her acquaintance fall out of their canoe, swim for a minute in different directions, and then both begin to drown. Being sure he can save only one, he lets his daughter drown and saves the other girl. Asked why, he says either (a) he was ever so slightly surer of being able to reach the acquaintance in time, or (b) the acquaintance was well on her way to being a brilliant scientist, bound to contribute more to the general happiness than his daughter and given that he could not save both, the choice he made produced more positive value. What do we think of this father? Would we want to shake his hand, or tell the story in the local paper as a moral lesson? Is he not a great fool, an object of pity and contempt? Indeed, this is the kind of incident we are embarrassed even to talk about, unlike the more human cases of moral heroism or gross selfishness.

If he had been in the canoe with the acquaintance and had sacrificed his own life instead of his daughter's, in order to save the acquaintance, we might feel awe, but not contempt or pity. Therefore the bad emotion we feel in the first case cannot be explained in terms of the father's sacrifice of self-interest, for there is a greater sacrifice of self-interest in the second case and we do not feel that emotion in the second case. A natural explanation is that the father owes something to his daughter that he does not owe to an acquaintance or a stranger. It is easy to say, "Yes, of course, we have special obligations to our children: utility is maximized if each takes care of his own." In general, I think most "brightening-your-own-corner-betters-the-world" arguments are naive or disingenuous. More to the present case, I do not think such a belief can begin to explain the contempt and embarrassment; besides, the case in which the father lets his daughter drown is one that does maximize expected utility.

It is not just that people are as a matter of fact blindly loyal or biased toward various social units, this being a fact of human nature we lament; rather, loyalty behavior elicits approbation and opposite behavior typically elicits guilt in the agent and disapproval in observers. The contempt we feel toward traitors is not unlike what we feel toward the father who lets his daughter drown. Our loyalties are values that contribute to what we think we should do, all things considered. Therefore they can compete with what are called considerations of social morality. This is even more plausible if, as I shall suggest, every group loyalty creates and grounds a domain of social morality. When these loyalties themselves are challenged in the name of social morality, the wider obligations determined by a wider loyalty are being asserted to have greater moral authority. As in any case of conflicting normative considerations, sometimes a person will judge his family or national obligations to take precedence over wider ones and sometimes he will not. It depends, among other things, on how much is at stake in each domain, on the possibiliy of a given action satisfying both loyalties to differing degrees, and on the "strengths" of the loyalties themselves.

This line of argument applies to all types of loyalty if it applies to any. The implication is that patriotic considerations are, for people who have a basis for patriotism, genuinely normative considerations, partly determinative of what they should do, all things considered.

I think that as a matter of fact all moral codes, at their roots, rest on self-dependent principles. Moral and evaluative principles are accepted because they serve one's kind, under some description or other, and they appear objective and impersonal only because they apply impartially within their domains, that is, within the moral communities they help define. Anything else would be branded by everyone as crazy and pointless: Logic allows me to value what is triangular or radially symmetrical and disvalue what is red or incandescent, and thereby have a set of values that is wholly impersonal and not in any respect self-dependent. But the egoism and group egoism of innately social, human animals will not allow perfect impartiality, indeed, cannot even find it intelligible.

Consequently I wish to suggest the following. Our wide and narrow loyalties define moral communities or domains within which we are willing to universalize moral judgments, treat equals equally, protect the common good, and in other ways adopt the familiar machinery of impersonal morality. For example, if I believe my family comes first when scarce resources or their safety is at stake, I am bound to universalize within my family: if one family member deserves a benefit so do the others unless some additional consideration applies to one but not to all of them. A loyalty defines a moral community in terms of a conception of a common good and a special commitment to fellow members of the group who share this good. The members, along with certain conventional, institutional structures, and often a geographical location, together constitute the community that is the object of my loyalty. Those who share this common good comprise my tribe; the common good is its flourishing, and this is why we acknowledge a system of social morality whose purpose is the safety and flourishing of the tribe and which applies impartially to its members.

I belong simultaneously to many "tribes" or moral communities, some of which include my family as a part and some of which do not. If the good of humanity as a moral end is species loyalty and not a shared ideal it will be like family loyalty and national loyalty: my species may not differ in any relevant respect from the invading Andromedans, just as my child may not differ in any relevant respect from George's child, yet in each case I will treat similar cases similarly only within the domain of what I have come to view as mine. This conception of my tribe, as distinct from a similar one, must be understood as an inherently historical notion: Its causal history defines it.

Social morality is impersonal and impartial when it confines itself to intra-tribal considerations, as when a parent, facing no challenge to family loyalty itself, seeks to do the right thing when interests conflict within his or her family. But when the national good competes with the good of one's family, the latter appears as a naked loyalty, and the former as social morality that demands impartial consideration of family and nonfamily. So too, nationalism in turn is a mere loyalty from the wider perspective of utilitarianism, but takes the form of impersonal, social morality in internal matters, including clashes with nested, narrower loyalties such as community or civic loyalty. This complexity probably did not face primitive Man and arises because modern Man belongs to many tribes at once.

According to this scheme every loyalty has the double aspect of being a self-dependent value in intersocietal competition and of grounding a system of impersonal, social morality for adjudicating intrasocietal conflicts. For example, when an academic department chairman apportions benefits and duties within the department he is guided by the common good of the department, which is taken for granted; what becomes at issue are fairness and relevant differences, as part of a system of social morality operating within a miniature moral community. But if the dean wants to give part of his budget to the English Department, department loyalty is exposed and competes with what the dean calls the common good, i.e., the good of the college. These are tribal conflicts—part of the dialectic of the ethics of parts and wholes—and the question arises whether all morality is tribal morality in this sense. If there was a widest loyalty and wide loyalties were the best ones, we might envisage a hierarchy. As we shall see, neither of these two claims can be shown to be true or even plausible.

To claim that all morality is tribal morality is not to deny that we value certain qualities in themselves. A loyalist favors a particular group under a certain description. But the description must be significant and concern such things as language, geography, culture, and the major activities of our lives. The explanation of what we find significant lies with the environmental and evolutionary determinants of human sociality. Moreover, people do not feel proud of just any features their community or nation possesses. We value in themselves certain features of a family, community, or nation which enter into our definition of its "flourishing." Such things as freedom, rationality, happiness, power, diversity, beauty, and detailed variants of these, seem to be valued

for their own sakes and to play a role in whether I
view some social unit as mine. Consequently, a
loyalist doesn't value something simply because it
is his. It must have features that make it worth
having, and it could deteriorate to the extent that
shame ultimately kills loyalty. But morality will
still be tribal morality if our tribes count for
more than other tribes with the same intrinsically
valued features.

Are even Kantians tribal moralists? Let us
grant that to a Kantian rational nature is an ideal,
valuable in itself, and ask instead whether there
are situations in which Kantians would be loyal to
some rational beings and not others. This is a
psychological question whose answer is not certain,
but a plausible answer would be importantly relevant
to the nature of human morality. Kant's Kingdom of
Ends is the assemblage of rational beings each of
which treats every member (including itself) as an
end and never a means. Beings who are not rational
beings can be treated as mere means because Kant
apparently had no conception of a still broader
moral community. Kantians seem to value rational
beings, not just "their" rational beings, and
suggesting that Kantians are group egoists requires
speculating about what they would say in hypothetical situations.

Someone who knew only his own family, other
individuals being solitary or machine-reared, might
say that families were of intrinsic worth, recognizing a loyalty to his own family only when he
encountered competing families. A philosophical
tribesman who knew only his own tribe might decide
that tribe members comprised a "kingdom of ends,"
having worth that hermits, exiles, and animals lack;
what is he to say when he discovers a dozen tribes,
some in competition with his own? What if human
space explorers were to encounter many rational
civilizations, all competing for resources as do the
different families and tribes we now encounter? I
suspect that a Kantian would come to think in terms
of our rational beings and their rational beings.
Rationality might remain an intrinsic value but be
subordinated to group egoism. A very wide loyalty
looks more like a pure ideal than does a narrow
loyalty because we haven't to decide what to think

of competitors. On this view all morality is tribal morality and there will be as many systems of social morality as there are loyalties.

Even if one could distill out of the totality of a person's values and principles a pure impersonal morality, nonetheless, effectively motivating people to be cooperative and non-predatory probably depends more on their coming to view their societies or "tribes" as their own. It is people's conscious group loyalties that enable civilized society to survive. There are many people who seem not to care much about their families, neighborhoods, cities, or various larger or different wholes. The effects of this attitude can range through indifference, automatic negative votes on tax and bond levies, cynical exploitation of the social services systems, vandalism, and crime. If what I have been saying about the nature and role of loyalties is correct, it will be socially useful to investigate what makes people perceive social units of various kinds as theirs.

This is a causal question of what, in a person's upbringing and environment, creates that expansion beyond self-interest, that making-one's-own, that generates loyalty, which in turn can motivate people to work and sacrifice for the good and safety of their societies. The obvious advantage of basing social morality on loyalties, as well as on ideals and rational self-interest, is that loyalty has discoverable social causes and we can make and test hypotheses about these causes. This is not obviously open to us when we base conscientious citizenship on either moral obligation or self-interest. If public morality and good citizenship are made to depend on obligation, on the language of duty and thou-shalt-nots, people will argue and rationalize about them, and they will become indignant when someone tries to tell them their duty. If social morality and citizenship are made to depend on self interest, most of society's appeals will rightly be perceived as sophistical. But if citizens are caused to perceive that what is in jeopardy is their so-and-so, they will care and sacrifice for it.

If a person does not view an institution, a family, a neighborhood, a nation, as in some sense his own, and yet we expect or think it is natural for him to do so, we can call him alienated. This is one meaning of alienation, more closely tied to our actual behavior and feelings than is the more abstract Marxist sense. In folksier terms we might say that he lacks a sense of national, municipal, or neighborhood pride, and to be proud of something implies connecting it with oneself, seeing it as one's own. I can be neither proud nor ashamed of an iceberg unless somehow I have been made to think of it as my iceberg. We do not call a stranger in New York alienated, at least not in the sense I mean. But a New Yorker can be alienated from his city for many different reasons and someone who visits the city can adopt it as his own and come to feel loyal to it.

Changes in our loyalties which over the long run we will be proud of are, hopefully, those elicited by knowledge, rationality, and sanity. These qualities, together with our basic emotions and our environments, cause us to view certain social entities as our own and to live at ease in them as well as feel committed to their good. At the most fundamental level, justifications of loyalties and ideals are impossible; in fact they aren't even interesting compared with evolutionary questions about what we have become predisposed to want, fear, and feel at ease in during a million years of Pleistocene and early Holocene tribal life.

4.4 <u>Consistent Egoism, Relatively Speaking.</u> We have seen that we need not universalize self-dependent normative judgments in what I called sense (1), that is, logic does not require the move from "I should save my child" to "I should save any similar child." But it is commonly argued that logic does require us to universalize in sense (3), from "I should save my child first" to "everyone should save his own child first." It is also argued that we are inconsistent when we do so. Plainly, the aim is to show that egoism is inconsistent. Whatever it shows will hold for any self-dependent judgment. If we ignore for just a moment an escape route that has to do with ethical relativism, it appears obvious why self-dependent judgments are

inconsistent when they are universalized. A
self-dependent judgment is <u>partial</u>: It says I
should do something because of its effect on me or
on what I view as mine; I cannot at the same time be
impartial, that is to say, allow the interests of
similar persons in similar circumstances to count
equally with what is mine. Either the fact that the
child, country or species is mine makes a difference
to what I should do, all things considered, or it
does not. Self-dependent judgments imply that it
does and when I universalize I imply that it does
not.

A universalization may be inconsistent with
other things I believe; a stronger claim is that a
self-dependent judgment and its universalization are
mutually inconsistent. The former, weaker claim
seems clearly true when we universalize ethical
egoism:

> (1)   Everyone ought to do what best serves
> his own interest.

> (2)   Max's shooting me would best serve his
> interest.

> .'. (3)   Max ought to shoot me.

(3) is inconsistent with other beliefs I almost
certainly hold, e.g., that Max ought not to shoot me.

Imagine that you found yourself holding down a
big spring-loaded lever. You are told that, at the
sound of a bell, if you let go your spouse would die
and if you continued to hold it down two total
strangers in Mongolia would die (and if you found a
way to do neither, all three would die). The lever
is spring-loaded in order to block arguments about
morally relevant differences between actions and
forebearances. We assume, among the three potential
victims, equal virtue, equally possible future
happiness, relatives equally ready to grieve, and
the rest. Which should you do? I think most people
would say that, all things considered, they would
save their spouses and moreover that they should.

Utilitarians, who upon calculating discover that
two is more than one and announce that they should

kill their spouses, would be declared by the great majority of Mankind to be fools and fanatics, to be less than human, not more. If utilitarians say, "Out of moral weakness I would kill the two strangers, but it would be wrong," they probably are lying, and if not lying then woefully insensitive to the difference between what they believe and what their theory tells them. I think that examples such as this show that we all know in our hearts that utilitarianism is perfectly silly. Hardly anyone thinks that, all things considered, he should value lives equally, regardless of their relation to himself and to his ideals. One might argue that the "should" that says to save one's spouse is prudential, not moral. But how does one defend that without begging the question? It is an all-things-considered "should," overriding all others, and such "shoulds" seem to be what ethics is about. Utility itself does not require that lives count equally; indeed, it implies that while you are most unlikely to count for more than one, you are very likely to count for less than one.

Someone in Mongolia is also holding down a lever, wired to your spouse and son. To universalize is to say, "if I ought to kill the two, then he ought to kill the two; I ought to kill the two, therefore he ought to kill my spouse and son." If you think you ought to kill his instead of yours and also think he ought to kill yours instead of his, it at least looks like an inconsistency.

The inconsistency that seems to follow from universalizing the non-utilitarian decision about the lever depends on the following inference:

      (a) He ought to kill my spouse instead of his.

.'. (b) My spouse ought to be killed instead of his.

Usually, when we believe things such as "H ought to release the lever" or "I should rescue the drowning woman," we also believe "the lever ought to be released" or "the drowning woman should be rescued." We go from "So-and-so ought to do A" to "A ought to be done (by at least somebody)." When we remove the reference to a particular agent we show that we mean the obligation impersonally. Here is an illustration of how the inconsistency depends on this inference. Imagine that Ayn Rand and I are two egoists who find ourselves in a one-egoist lifeboat. I say,

> (1) I ought to save myself and throw R to the sharks.

and then universalize to

> (2) R ought to save herself and throw me to the sharks.

I do not think that (1) and (2) can be shown to be formally inconsistent unless we take them to imply the impersonal judgments

> (3) I ought to be saved and R be thrown to the sharks.

and

> (4) R ought to be saved and I be thrown to the sharks.

So the ethical egoist, as well as those who hold patriotic, speciesist or other self-dependent principles, can universalize without inconsistency by denying the inference we usually make from "ought to do" to "ought to be." If he does, he must reject the question, "But which of you ought to be saved?", and if he does this he accepts a certain form of ethical relativism. For in rejecting that question he seems to mean that it is right _for_ _him_ to do what is necessary for himself to survive and right _for_ _R_ to do what is necessary for R to survive.

This move puts the egoist who universalizes in a position that contrasts sharply with the conception of value that is internal to a tribe, that is, that characterizes a moral community. When someone says world peace is his highest value he means it objectively and impersonally in the sense that there should be world peace: he means that world peace ought to exist and what produces it should be done if it is possible to do so. But when the egoist says the ultimate value is one's own happiness, he must mean something quite different if he is to be consistent. We must take him to mean that his own happiness is his highest value, R's happiness is R's highest value, but neither is the highest value: neither ought to exist, nothing is the highest value. The reference to who is doing the valuing cannot be eliminated and in this sense his judgments become irreducibly biographical. So, unless I relativize the "ought" in the sense explained I cannot claim that somebody ought to kill R without implying that R ought to be killed; if I allow that implication I cannot consistently claim that other people should be egoists too. Our usual move from "I ought to do it" to "It ought to be done" is not affected by the fact that sometimes only I ought to do it, in virtue of some special office, ability or relation I have. For instance, if the only police officer in town says, "I ought to investigate those screams," he thinks the screams ought to be investigated, even though he may also think only he has the obligation to do it.

In general, my willingness to move from "I ought to do X" to "X ought be done" depends on whom one is addressing. One Athenian may say to another Athenian "The Spartans ought to pay reparations for so-and-so." But he would not say this to a Spartan unless he were appealing to some principle he thought both of them were likely to share. He would not tell the Spartan "Athens ought not to be defeated," although he might say "I am morally obligated to fight you," and the Spartan might reply, "I understand." Usually, a self-dependent obligation is expressed in the impersonal mode only to those who share with the speaker ownership of whatever it is on which he bases the obligation. It is foolish and childish to tell someone "X ought to be saved because it is mine" when X is not also his, that is, when I cannot say instead "X ought to be saved because it is ours," whether X be my happiness, my family, my nation, or my species. In this respect ethical egoists, unlike loyalists, have no one to talk to and this may be a reason why some philosophers think egoism is not a moral position.

Relativistic "oughts" are appropriate when truly alien self-dependent judgments confront one another;

when they do there is no plausible alternative to saying "It is right for us that we save ours first and it is right for them that they save theirs first." It is the most appropriate thing to say in answer to the question, "What ought the Mongolian to do with his lever?" It is the correct response of the ethical egoist when he is asked what other people should do. He does not hold the inconsistent view that he ought to be sacrificed for other people, and he cannot take seriously the claim that the only obligation of others is to sacrifice themselves for him. Moreover, he knows that his answer to the question, "What should other people do?" should not be just, "Nothing." Yet it is not that what is right for me and what is right for the Andromedan count equally or that neither is "really right"; to say that is to forget who one is: to whom are they supposed to count equally? To a rock, or to an "ideal observer" who loves nothing? When Aristotle distinguished "the good for man" from "the good for a vegetable," nobody accused him of implying that these two goods, when they clash at dinner time, count equally. Functional theories of ethics such as Aristotle's are self-dependent ones. Aristotle, I am sure, would have reminded us that he is a human, not a vegetable and not an impartial observer of humans and vegetables.

Moral judgments in the impersonal, nonrelative mode presuppose a community that shares certain principles, that is, a moral community within which reasons can be expected to have a general appeal. My position differs from a somewhat related one recently put forth by Gilbert Harman in THE NATURE OF MORALITY.[1] Harman says, "someone ought to do something only if he has a reason to do it" and that "our moral principles are binding only on those who share them or whose principles give them reasons to accept them." His view implies it is false that a hardened professional killer ought not to kill people, for the killer has no reason not to kill people. This is counterintuitive, as Harman admits; but it also readmits the moral subjectivism he wishes to avoid if we never can say what someone who disagrees with us on a deep level should or shouldn't do. A main function of morality is to place prohibitions and obligations on deviant and potentially deviant individuals within the moral community. It is essential to the viability of a moral community that it not be too easy to opt out of it. So it is self-defeating to define the moral community as those who agree with us.

On my view we can claim that the hardened professional killer ought not to kill people not because our reasons appeal to the killer but because they have a general appeal, and serve the common good, within the community in which he and we live. We can say what he shouldn't do because he, unlike the Andromedan, is a member of our tribe, however deviant or renegade: He may be alienated but he is not alien. On the same grounds we can censure ethical egoists and ordinary delinquents, whatever they may think about it. Most of us, after all, think that what the egoist sanctions is often wrong and ought not to be done.

One form of moral decadence is to view every person as ethical egoists view each other, or as we might view invading Andromedans. When we do this all "oughts" are relative "oughts," and we can only speak of what is immoral for Harry (when his principles imply it is) and not immoral for Max (when his principles imply it isn't). Each person is viewed only as an autonomous individual, as a moral community of one member rather than as a member of a moral community. The ultimate source of this variety of decadence is failure to understand or accept the essentially coercive nature of morality. If we cannot say that a person morally ought to do something unless, on a deep level at least, he already agrees with us, then everyone becomes the Andromedan. Harman's principle, that someone morally ought to do something only if he has a reason to do it, is decadent in the sense I have in mind. If the professional killer ought to quit killing only if it follows from his own principles that he ought, then if he disagrees with me he is making a logical or factual error: We disagree only about what it is his principles tell him to do. Harman's claim implies that moral disagreement is really disagreement about the content of the killer's "values system." However, in a morally healthy society, the ability of people within the moral community to make, and make felt, non-relative moral judgments depends only on what the community knows, reasons, and feels, not on the beliefs of its malefactors and miscreants. Otherwise morality will not be a sufficiently cohesive social force.

The problem, for which there is no simple answer, is to pin-point the difference between deviants such as the professional killer, about whom we can make impersonal "ought" judgments, and aliens, such as Andromedans, foreign patriots, and other children's parents, about whom we cannot. The complexity of the ethics of parts and wholes--of the relations between our nested loyalties--shows itself in our willingness to employ relative "oughts" about a person regarding one kind of relation he bears to us, and simultaneously employ impersonal "oughts" in other relations he may bear to us. I may say that Harry ought, in the relative sense, to save his own family ahead of mine; and that he ought, in the impersonal sense, to pay his taxes.

We often come to expand our conception of our tribe on the basis of features we discover we share with others. Thus education can bring a person to care equally for members of his race and other races; but it is not likely to make him care equally for members of his family and other families. The expansion of one's moral horizon is a function of interests that are at stake as well as knowledge. In some cases these interests may generate relatively narrow loyalties that are forever in conflict with the universal levelling of the utilitarians. It is of the nature of a self-dependent value that it may, and then again it may not, be immune to increased knowledge of similarities and differences.

4.5   Golden Rule Arguments.   In Matt. 7:12 Christ said, "Therefore all things whatsoever ye would that men should do to you, do ye even so to them." There is a temptation to interpret this as just a version of the universalizability principle. If the Golden Rule were an actual test for right and wrong it would seem to go as follows: If I want to know if I should do so-and-so to Harry I ask if I would that Harry do so-and-so to me; if I would, then I should do it to him. If what I "would that he do to me" means what I want him to do to me, the Golden Rule will justify countless immoral actions: If I would have others satisfy my indolence, cowardice, or masochistic sexual desires, then I should do likewise for them. Consequently, this reasoning goes, we should take Christ to be making a conditional, conceptual point, like a good analytical philosopher: "What is right for you to do to others is in similar circumstances right for others to do to you." The "would that men should do to you" is understood as "right that ..." and not as "what you desire that ...." On this view the Golden Rule cannot tell you what to do until it is coupled with substantive moral rules such as the Decalogue or the ethical teachings in the New Testament.

Along with many philosophers I think that is the wrong interpretation and that the Golden Rule was meant to test the morality of desires by universalizing them. I also think that the Golden Rule is a plausible test of right and wrong only in its restricted or negative form. The restricted form says, "Do not do to others what you do not want them to do to you," which is the Silver Rule of Confucius. It is more plausible than the Golden Rule because it only presupposes a community of persons with similar basic aversions, whereas the Golden Rule presupposes a community of persons with similar basic wants and aversions.

Kant and Richard Hare build on the negative or "Confucian" version of the Golden Rule. They do so in arguments that appeal only to desires and not to goods or evils, and this, on a certain level, allows their arguments to be a _priori_. Thus Hare's schema for moral reasoning in FREEDOM AND REASON can be laid out in simplifed form as follows.[2]

> (1) I have an overriding aversion to Freda's hanging me.

> .'. (2) I cannot accept the prescription "Let Freda hang me."

> .'. (3) I cannot accept that Freda ought to hang me.

> .'. (4) I cannot accept that in similar circumstances I ought to hang Freda.

Telescoping the argument we get, "I cannot accept that I should do X to F if I have an overriding aversion to F's doing X to me," which is the Silver Rule. Given that I do not want Freda to X me, I say to myself "I should not X Freda," but this normative judgment is not an entailment of the argument, thus allowing it to be a priori without violating Hume's Law of no "oughts" from "is's." A crucial difficulty with this argument and with Kant's very similar argument is that some people's all-things-considered aversions are very different from those of the rest of us. The tests for right and wrong that Kant and Hare devise each run into this difficulty, so the criticisms I shall make of Kant will, with some changes, apply to Hare too.

Kant limits moral concern to the domain of rational beings, to beings whose self-interested or appetitive nature (expressed in maxims) is morally constrained by their rational nature (expressed in the requirement to universalize and avoid contradictions in will). Kant's system is profoundly antithetical to utilitarianism not because it judges actions by their natures instead of by their consequences--this being a superficial dichotomy, as we shall see in Chapter Five--, but because the ultimate basis of morality is rationality and not the absence of suffering. Animals who lack rationality but who are capable of suffering can, it seems, be treated by us as "mere means" and not as ends in themselves. Or should we say that cows have a small degree of rationality, generating weak obligations toward them? Even if a Kantian could justify humane treatment of animals on the basis of their partial rationality, this would invite research into breeding food animals without brains (but with enough ganglia to permit them to live and suffer). Would this, for a Kantian, constitute a final solution to the veal calf problem? Utilitarians, with their preoccupation with getting "pleasure" (whatever that is) and avoiding suffering, can more easily than Kant expand their moral concern to veal calves and chickens, whereas Kant, more than the utilitarians, can morally prepare us for the arrival of the rational Andromedans.

The categorical imperative seems to yield moral conclusions by the purest magic, without appealing to substantive principles. This is just appearance: The assumed intrinsic value of rational beings establishes the moral domain within which I am asked to universalize. Kant begins with a maxim, which is a policy statement, already universal, that says I may do such-and-such a kind of action because it has results I want--getting out of financial difficulties, sparing myself the trouble of helping others, and so on. All Kantian maxims specify action for the sake of an end I want; most are selfish, self-dependent principles, although some may be based on virtuous inclinations. I want or "will" to act on immoral maxims because they put what is mine ahead of what is yours and thereby specify ends I want. Equally obviously, I am not willing for you to act on the corresponding universal laws if they put what is yours ahead of mine and thereby specify ends I do not want. If my maxim is that I may make false promises to get out of financial trouble, the corresponding universal law is that every rational being may do that. When my maxim aims at benefitting myself or mine ahead of other rational beings, then I will want the advantage of my acting on such a maxim and I will be averse to others acting on it and putting what is theirs ahead of mine.

Now there is nothing contradictory or irrational per se about my wanting a certain action performed if it is done by me and not wanting that action if it is done by others. They are different actions. But if, as Kant claims, one's conception of how a perfectly rational being would judge requires that if I affirm the one (the maxim) I must affirm the other (the universal law), and if, moreover, affirming a maxim or any practical principle includes willing it in the sense of wanting that it be carried out, then Kant is able to claim that my rational nature requires, in the case of such maxims, that I simultaneously will what I want and what I do not want.

This is the contradiction in will. It is a natural and obvious result of universalizing self-dependent principles, including, of course, self-interested ones. If I believe that I shall (or may, or should) protect something of mine at other people's expense, I am favorably disposed to doing so and ill-disposed to others doing the same thing at my expense. Kant's position is that respect for our rational nature requies that we universalize our maxims and if, when we do so, we would end up willing what we want and don't want at the same time, then that maxim is an immoral one. There is nothing puzzling about the fact that some practical principles give rise to clashing volitions if they are universalized. For self-dependent judgments and policies, whether selfish or not, let what is mine count for more than yours and their universalization lets what is yours count for more than mine.

But must we universalize our maxims, and hence must we accept the corresponding universal law if we accept the maxim? Of course we must, within the boundary of a moral community that sets the limits of our moral concern. But reason alone cannot determine the boundary. Kant asks me to expand my conception of my tribe to include not just members of my family, my countrymen, or my species, but all rational beings (another description of his kind). This is Kant's moral leap. Neither reason nor the idea of my rational nature requires that if I may do so-and-so then any rational being may do so-and-so; reason is equally compatible with my claiming that if I may do it then any fellow citizen may do it or any sentient creature may do it. Reason, or as Kant puts it, rational nature, need not have as its object of respect only itself. Thinking that it does is the fundamental mistake that disguises the substantive moral assumption behind the categorical imperative and leads Kant to think that the foundation of morality is a priori. Kant's mistake is thinking that the universal judging and willing that rationality requires of the moral subject, and which may well be a priori, implies that respect for rational nature as an object of moral concern is equally a priori. It turns on an ambiguity of the expression "respect for rationality," or better, on conflating the moral subject's respect for rational procedure with rational nature as an object of respect.

When Kant speaks of the "law-like judging" to which a purely rational being would confine itself he means it would be inconsistent or at least irrational not to universalize one's maxims. But when he speaks of rational nature as an end he means instead that we must give absolute moral value to all rational beings. Thus the third formulation of the categorical imperative says "So act so to treat humanity, whether in thine own person or in that of any other, in every case as an end withal, never as means only." Here he states the domain of moral concern, within which similar cases must be judged similarly: policies or principles we accept for ourselves are ones we are rationally bound to accept for all bearers of rational nature.

The ambiguity in the notion of respect for rationality allows us to distinguish formal from substantive claims in Kant's ethics in the following way. When Kant speaks of respect for how a rational being would judge, he is, as we have seen, speaking of the requirement to judge similar cases similarly, within a domain whose boundaries are laid down independently of this formal requirement. Kant could equally insist on respect for rationality in this sense if he were a rational egoist, required to judge in a law-like way and hence to make similar egoistic judgments in similar circumstances; or if he believed all conscious beings must be treated as ends, never as means, and therefore that what he wills he may do he must will bats and cats may do. Respect for rationality in this first sense is simply universalizability and is blind to what counts as a relevant feature of a being. Respect for rationality in the second sense is the idea of rational nature as an object of respect, that is, as a thing of value which must be treated as an end and never as a mere means. Respect for rationality in the first sense is respect for rational procedure, and does not imply respect for rationality in the second sense, which is respect for rational nature. The requirement that respect lays on us may be a priori in the first sense, but it is not a priori in the second sense.

One of the problems faced by everyone who teaches Kant concerns the tough character who, while strolling past poor Max who is in quicksand, can will that everyone including himself be left in the quicksand if he is weak or stupid enough to fall in. He can will his maxim to be a universal law because he is more averse to weakness than to death. The problem for Kant is exactly that posed

by Richard Hare's "fanatic," that is, the problem of
the Nazi who can accept that he send Jews to death
camps, because he is more averse to Jews walking
around freely than he is to being sent to a death
camp, in the hypothetical situation in which he is a
Jew.[3]

Ordinary people want to do selfish things they
would not want done generally in similar circumstances. The paramount role of moral argument in
Kant is to block attempts to justify such acts (as
distinct from public policy issues such as abortion
and atomic weapons). It is to immoral selfishnes
that Kantian and Kantian type arguments are
addressed. They are right on target, but they
presuppose a community of persons with normal wants
and aversions. Autonomous or self-legislative moral
arguments do not work on freaks, on people who are
more opposed to weakness, or Jews, or dancing, than
they are to being killed. Neither do they, from our
point of view, always work on Amish, Nagas, or
Arapesh, much less the Andromedans, though they may
work for Andromedans within their own moral community. Finally, Kantian and neo-Kantian arguments
do not work on moral revolutionaries, today's
"freaks" who may be tomorrow's idealistic martyrs.
These outsiders are created by the philosophers'
search for the lowest common denominator of rational
acceptability, which accounts for the sense of petit
bourgeois conservatism and cautiousness one gets on
reading the neo-Kantian theories of writers such as
Richard Hare and John Rawls. The basic problem is
that common rationality is not enough. There would
have to be universal all-things-considered wants and
fears for there to be a universal autonomous
morality, and these we do not have, not even within
a single moral community.

But it is enough--indeed, it is a great accom-
plishment--for Kant to have generated arguments that
can apply cogently to the commonplace doings of
ordinary people. If someone just doesn't care, or
doesn't mind, what we very much care about and mind,
we cannot reach him, he is beyond the pale. And why
must we be able to reach everyone? There are bad
people whom we often can reason with and there are
monsters and fanatics; there is a place for
reasoning and argument and a place for wordless

force and self-defense. An argument that depends on our caring whether or not we are shot or burned to a crisp loses no cogency for us just because it cannot move another person who does not care whether he is shot or burned to a crisp.

Partiality for what is <u>one's</u> <u>own</u> is to be found at the roots of every system of morality and it ultimately determines what features of things count as relevant ones. The notion of a totally impartial universalizer is ultimately incoherent. He may be impartial relative to the conflicting interests of the participants in a given dispute, much as an arbitrator in a labor dispute or an international court in a fishing rights dispute, but he could not be impartial at all levels of possible controversy. The philosophical idea of a totally impartial, ideal universalizer is a fraud because even when we suppose him to be God, we necessarily suppose he counts, as relevant, whatever impartially benefits members of our kind. And this is not the end of the matter since <u>what</u> we fancy God to think of as our kind--conscious beings, rational beings, human beings, or American beings--, is ultimately less a matter of reason and knowledge than a matter of what causes have worked upon us. If God were toally impartial He would not have any morality, not even regarding His own good; He would have no basis whatever for favoring the good of human beings over that of Andromedan bacteria or African tsetse flies.

4.6 <u>The Possibility of Selfishness.</u> How are self-dependent normative judgments possible? When I make one I apply the crucial indexical term ("my ache, my child, my country") to just one of two things I know could be exactly similar. The question will lead us into issues about the metaphysics of the self. It is commonly thought that selfishness is the natural state of goal-seeking entities and that altruism is either impossible or requires some special explanation. Philosophers and theologians argue that only a human being can act on universal, impartial policies, policies I will loosely call Kantian policies. Until very recently, the view was echoed by evolutionary biologists on the grounds that motives and tendencies selected for in evolution are selfish ones that better enable individuals to survive and

103

pass on their genes. The truth of the matter, I suggest, is the other way around: The "natural state" of goal-seeking entities is to act on Kantian, altruistic policies and egoism is harder to account for than altruism.

Imagine that Robert Kraut$_1$ is the product of a cloning experiment: Until age twenty, Kraut$_1$ and his genetically identical replica, Kraut$_2$, were raised in laboratory environments 100 miles apart in which the two of them always had exactly similar stimuli and other causal inputs, in identical temporal sequences. They were, as we say, numerically distinct but qualitatively exactly similar, right down to every thought and sensation occurring in them.

Each gets a severe toothache. Now at least one aspect of the morality of coping with these toothaches is obvious: Whatever moral grounds we the observers have for relieving one toothache we also have for relieving the other. For scientific reasons we might decide to cure just one toothache and observe what happens, but we would not have moral grounds for deciding which one to cure. (There might be other grounds, e.g., Kl's lab is more easily staffed, that arise from differences in the environments of the replicas and which are not removable without postulating replica universes.) To be sure, one of them is Kl and the other is K2, one in _this_ lab and the other in _that_ lab, but as we have seen, singular terms such as "Kl" and "this" do not indicate dissimilarities and hence do not indicate morally relevant dissimilarities.

Each is aware that he has a replica with a toothache. The loudspeaker asks Kl (and another asks K2), "Whose toothache should we cure? We will only cure one." Kl shouts, "Mine, not his! The pain is terrible!" Now _that_'s egoism, and a clear case of a self-dependent normative judgment. Kl knows that K2 has a toothache exactly as painful as his own, but he nonetheless can make differing evaluations of the two, evaluations equally informed observers cannot make because the toothaches do not differ. We want to say, of course, that the two aches are different "for Kl" in a way in which they are not different "for the observers"; but we know they are exactly similar. This should be puzzling; for we should remember that Kl has no information the observers lack, and yet egoistic value judgments are often said to be rational ones. We need to understand better what a selfish judgment is based on, by which I mean understand whatever mental discriminations (perceptions or intelligent processes) from which it would make sense to say Kl's selfish judgment flowed. There is, I believe, a difficulty in understanding the very idea of selfishness (or egoism), especially when it is compared, as it will be shortly, with the kinds of policies on which machines and lower organisms are able to act. The question is a transcendental one: How is selfishness possible, for it is a plain fact that people are often selfish.

While Kl cannot point to a difference between Kl and K2 (if he could, we could), he can tell the difference between a toothache of Kl and a toothache of K2 in a way in which we cannot; he can appraise or value toothaches according to whether they are his or another's. And the self-dependent nature of his judgment is irreducible. He does not just numerically individuate them as two--observers can do that. He does not base his judgment on the claim that one ache is felt and other is unfelt: Both are felt. Neither will it suffice for him to say "One ache is felt by Kl and not by K2," without further specification of which one Kl is. He must say "One ache is felt by me," if he is to make his judgment intelligible.

A hypothesis emerges from this. Egoism and impersonal morality depend on different concepts of the self. Egoism depends on what I call a concept of the self as a particular; it involves the capacity to discriminate among particulars that might be exactly similar, to identify one of those particulars as oneself, and to base wants, evaluations, and policies on this discrimination. It is the ability to comprehend and accept what I have called self-dependent judgments. Entities that lack this concept of the self cannot act on egoistic policies.

Impersonal morality depends on a concept of the self as (an instance of) a kind of thing; here Kl identifies himself for evaluative purposes in terms of sets of features which, in principle, K2 or other things could also have. He takes the "Kantian point of view," and therefore cannot judge that you should cure his toothache rather than K2's. K1's impersonal value judgments are based on reasons which, in principle, any observer could understand and accept in the same way K1 understands them.

"Concept of the self as a particular" and "concept of the self as a kind" are expressions of convenience that require further explanation. When I act on an impersonal, universal policy, I treat myself as an instance of a kind, for example, an instance of a thief or a thing with a toothache. An instance of a $\emptyset$ is, of course, a particular. But the point is, in terms of this policy I do not view myself differently from any other instance; I just pick out one more case of a $\emptyset$, which happens to be me. Only the kind I represent is relevant to my judgment or action. But when I have a concept of the self as a particular it matters, and affects my judgment, which instance or particular of a given kind I identify: it matters whether or not the instance is me. So the difference between these two "concepts" or ways of viewing the self is the difference between basing a judgment on picking out myself as just another particular which is $\emptyset$, and basing a judgment on my being a particular instance of $\emptyset$ and not just any $\emptyset$--a particular particular, as it were--, namely the one that is me.

So the first part of the answer to the trans-cendental question, "How is selfishness possible?", is that only an entity with a concept of the self as a particular can have selfish policies. Which raises the question of what kind of entity can have a concept of the self as a particular. I want to suggest that whereas any entity that can be said to follow policies can act on the basis of the kinds it belongs to, only to a conscious entity can it matter which particular of a given kind it is.

A simplified, intuitive basis for my claim about consciousness and the idea of the self as a particular is seen in the example of K1 and his cloned replica K2. When K1 says "Me first," does he distinguish himself from K2 only numerically?

Egoism would be incomprehensible, simply crazy, if this were all we could say in explanation of it: Why prefer one "this" over another? And why prefer the one that is himself to K2, if all that can be said is that the egoist (mysteriously) prefers one of two numerically distinct but qualitatively exactly similar particulars? But there is, of course, a way in which a person can differentiate one particular from another without either noting a feature that one has and the other lacks or mentioning the spatial/temporal predicates that numerically individuate them. He feels the one pain but not the other. This is a basis that a person and presumably any conscious entity has for differentiating two particulars without having to note a feature that belongs to one but not the other. He knows that K1 is in pain and he also knows that K2 is in pain. But the pain that is his (and the person that is himself) is more important to him because, and only because, it is the one he feels. The separation of conscious states into those that are one's own and those that are not provides a third way (and the egoist's way) of distinguishing among particulars, the first being to notice differences in qualities or features and the second to apprehend different spatial/temporal predicates.

Imagine a simple kind of robot: A box on wheels with mechanical arms, sensors for touch, radio waves, colors, etc., and the capacity to translate radioed instructions into appropriate action. It can be built with present day technology and I shall assume it is not conscious, or not more likely to be conscious than a cruise missile. If we populate a town with these robots, of different sorts but including two that are exactly alike, and we radio to one of the two (R1), "Shoot robots with flashing green lights," R1 will do that. If R1's sensors can see that it is a robot with flashing green lights it will shoot itself as readily as any.

Can we successfully give R1 the instruction, "Oil thyself"? Upon hearing this, on what basis does R1 pick out the right robot to oil? Is it like the basis K1 has for treating his own toothache first, or is it like the basis the robot has for acting on "Shoot robots with flashing green lights"? We could easily give R1 the latter kind of basis by building it to treat the sentence "Oil thyself" as equivalent to "Oil blue robots" (it is the only blue one), or "Oil robots whose oil hole sensors send a $\emptyset$ type 'Keep oiling!' signal" (and only its own oil hole sensor sends $\emptyset$ type "Keep oiling!" signals). Doing this would be to make it translate "Oil thyself" into a universal rule which, as a matter of contingent fact, applies only to itself. The "thyself" would not be an egocentric particular for Rl but code for a set of repeatable features.

On reflection, "Oil thyself" seems to be wholly unmanageable by my robot unless it is treated by it as shorthand for general or universal directions (these directions, we humans can go on to say, having been tailored by us to apply only to a single individual). But not only is no such translation into universal directions necessary for the person Kl, it is difficult to see how any such translation of Kl's egoistic policy is possible. "My ache should be cured" cannot be translated into feedback statements about the neurological system because, first, whose neurological system do the statements about feedback refer to? "Cure ache that causes neural process X" plainly won't do even as an analogue of "Cure my ache" since the owner of neural process X is unspecified. Second, if neurological causal claims provide a basis for Kl's egoistic judgment, that basis is as accessible to an observer as it is to Kl himself; but Kl's basis cannot also serve as an observer's basis.

We can, of course, imagine ten non-conscious robots fighting over the oil spigot, a perfect picture of "selfish" behavior. But the logic of their behavior is different: They act on policies that are universal and therefore nonegoistic, but which apply only to themselves because we built them that way. Their behavior is no more egoistic, in the sense I am examining, than is that of the impartial person who resolves to give the money to whomever has characteristic $\emptyset$ and then discovers that only he has $\emptyset$. In such cases the robot and the person serve themselves only _per accidens_.

There are entities, of which robots are illustrations, which necessarily are perfect Kantians.

Kant said that perfectly rational beings, like God, would necessarily act only on universal laws and not need morality. I am offering another reason why an entity might necessarily act only on universal laws; namely when it is an entity that lacks a concept of the self as a particular. Robots Rl and R2 cannot discriminate between themselves and others, when it comes to doing harm or benefit, except on the basis of differences between them that they perceive or react to. This is compatible, perhaps even identical, with altruism of the sort Christ asserted: "Love thy neighbor as thyself"; but it is incompatible with egoism. An implication of my hypothesis is that exclusive altruism, in the sense of regarding only other people's good to the exclusion of one's own, requires a concept of the self as a particular as much as does egoism.

It may be objected that non-conscious entities lack a concept of the self altogether. Related to this is the objection that non-conscious entities cannot act, they just react; they cannot follow policies, they follow programs; they do not distinguish or perceive, they respond differentially. Part of the answer is that I want to grant as much as possible to those who say machines can be like us: intelligent, goal-seeking, etc. But in any case, many intelligence-attributing words such as "goal," "purpose," "policy," and "perceive" can apply to a non-conscious entity in senses that are natural enough given its structure and behavior, but without forcing us to conclude that the thing feels. And attributing to robots the idea of the self as an instance of various kinds is not altogether unnatural because my robot can pick out itself, albeit defeasibly, on the basis of clusters of features and thus be programmed to do certain things to itself in certain circumstances.

My hypothesis may sound incredible: that the possibility of selfishness is limited to human beings and others which, like human beings, have a certain concept of the self which in turn depends on having consciousness; and that some lower creatures and inferior robots cannot act on selfish policies. Philosophy, ethology, and until very recently, evolutionary theory, have taught the opposite: that lower animals fight tooth and claw out of total selfishness and that only human beings (and other higher creatures like God and angels) are capable of altruism and self-sacrifice. A typical view was that of Thomas Henry Huxley,[4] who argued in "Evolution and Ethics" in 1893 that Man's biological nature, being a product of natural selection, was totally selfish, whereas Man's ethical nature, since it was capable of altruism, had to have a spiritual component that transcended evolution.

Consider an example in terms of which we can take a closer look at the argument.

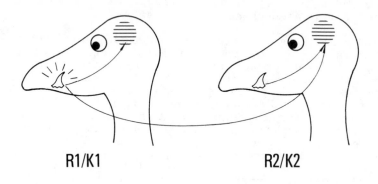

R1/K1   R2/K2

Imagine these exactly similar entities first as persons (K1 and K2) and then as non-conscious robots (R1 and R2). Let K2 be an egoist who says "I should cure only my toothache." A nerve is strung from K1's tooth to K2's brain, and moreover it connects in K2's brain exactly where his own tooth connects. The likely effect of this is that when K2 feels a toothache he will, in the usual sense in which we can locate the place of pain, "feel it in" his own tooth, whether it is his own rotten tooth or K1's rotten tooth that is causing the pain.

K2's policy is to cure the pain he is conscious of and which (tautologously, perhaps) is his pain and not another's. The cause could be his tooth or

Kl's tooth and he could be mistaken as to which tooth caused his toothache. But if his policy is to cure the pain he feels, then it is not possible that the same policy should also direct him to cure a similar pain of someone else, however much it might direct him to fix someone else's tooth and incidentally result in curing someone else's pain.

Now imagine that our two entities are non-conscious robots instead of persons and a mechanical tooth sends a malfunction signal to R2's electronic "brain." We could build R2 to be able to receive the signal only from its own tooth, and to repair only its own. Nonetheless, whatever kind of signal it got from its own tooth it could, logically, get from Rl's, and a sufficiently clever parasite robot could present its own tooth for repair by K2. What I envisage is a parasite robot that always could interfere mechanically or tap into R2's electronics, so as to present another instance of the kind of cues that make R2 repair itself, although in this case R2 would repair the parasite. Up to a point, the same is true of a person: Whatever signal K2 got from his own tooth he could, logically, get from Kl's, and so on. But what policy of R2 would be functionally equivalent to K2's policy to cure his pain (as distinct from fix his tooth)?

In reply, perhaps we should understand selfish responses of both persons and robots as causal effects of their internal states. Let us hypothe-size that making a selfish judgment is just responding to a stimulus. An organ is prodded and it contracts, a robot senses an oil lack and it oils itself, a person has pain and tends himself or says "Cure me." A cause operates on a particular entity, not a kind of entity, and the effect is self-tending behavior. When K2's tooth hurts him certain effects occur and these can include his uttering or thinking "I should cure my ache," just as, when an organ is prodded or a circuit activated, certain behavior is caused. Ought we to conclude that a robot has an impartial policy when it says, "Oil blue ones," and the functional equivalent of an egoistic policy when it is simply caused by its internal states to begin self-oiling motions? On this view, a robot analogue of "Cure my toothache pain" is something like, "Make the tooth malfunction signal cease"; in other words, it aims at making its internal machine state cease. Is the malfunction signal like the pain?

Up to a point, this is my own view of selfish behavior. On the dispositional theory, egoistic judgments are replacement egoistic behavior. K1's utterance, "Cure mine first," is the effect of an internal cause in a particular individual. Nevertheless, the kind of selfish policy a conscious entity can have remains unique: The cause of my selfish judgment is a conscious state. Only my own conscious states can affect me in the way in which they do (another tautology, perhaps). So it is false that _any_ cause of the same kind can have the effect in question. The robot, however, responds in the prescribed way to any cause that affects it with the right repeatable (electronic) characteristics, making its policy an impartial one. Thus it will not do to say that, for a machine, an egoistic judgment is a response to a particular state of the system and an impartial judgment is a reponse to a repeatable feature that may or may not be part of the system: If the particular state of the system is a machine state, then any particular state will do, whether it belongs to itself or another, so long as it has the same causal role. For this reason we always can invent ingenious parasite robots that supply that cause by infiltrating R2 and substituting their own circuits for R2's, so that R2 responds to a state of the parasite instead of to a state of itself. But a human egoist's policy, because it is aimed (ultimately) at the egoist's own feelings and states of consciousness, cannot possibly be activated similarly by the feelings of another person. K2 cannot have a parasite that substitutes pains or other conscious states and thereby gets K2 to respond because it feels the parasite's pain.

There appears to be a sense in which a person can be mistaken and the robot cannot: R2 is following its program just as truly when it fixes its parasite's tooth or circuit as when it fixes its own. To claim that R2 _mistakenly_ repairs its parasite instead of itself appears to assume illegitimately that something in its program is inherently directed toward itself. When we ask, "Whose tooth does R2's policy aim at fixing?", the answer is, "Whoever owns the tooth that sends the appropriate malfunction signals." When we ask, "Whose ache does K2's policy aim at curing," the answer is, "His own." Hence, we cannot give R2 a concept of the self as a particular, we can merely program it to respond in a certain way to a given kind of stimulus.

My treatment of these attempts at machine/human parallels may prompt what seems to be a more basic objection, namely that I mix up "functional" and "structural/causal" accounts of human and robot behavior. On one level, the functional, "Oil thyself" and "Cure your own ache" are directives that say what they are to do without saying anything about how, causally speaking, they do it. On the other level, "Such and such a chain of neurophysiological and other bodily causes takes place" and "such and such a chain of electrical and other physical causes takes place" describe how, causally speaking, they do what they are to do. The objection is that I illegitimately contrast functional accounts of human behavior with structural/causal accounts of robot behavior.

If by a structural/causal account one means a causal account in terms of the subject matter of physics, I agree that such an account of a person's behavior would show him to be no different from a nonconscious robot, for the obvious reason that conscious states are not part of the subject matter of physics. I have, however, let K2's pain sensation count as a state or occurrence that is part of an account, even a causal one, of his behavior. I have not assumed that the pain gets mentioned only in "functional" or purposive descriptions but drops out of a causal one. For it really isn't very interesting to discover that if human policies are explained without mentioning conscious states they are just like the policies of non-conscious entities.

My suggestion, minimally, is that there are implications for ethics and for the kind of concept of the self an entity can have that depend on how one describes that entity. Only if one describes a conscious entity in terms of its conscious states, which seems natural enough to do, will egoistic policies be ascribable to it. So how a human being is described makes a difference.

4.7 <u>Super Individuals and Group Egoism.</u> The sociobiologist Edward O. Wilson has discussed what he calls "the morality of the gene."[5] Genes, Wilson says, are completely selfish in the sense that they cause behavior and somatic structures that "aim" only at maximizing chances of the genes' replication in future generations. The happiness of the individual organisms whose behavior genes predispose, indeed, of anything besides what affects the likelihood of their replication, means nothing to them. Yet, individual genes or gene "tokens" are perfect Kantians: An instance of a gene "aims" at the proliferation of its kind and is indifferent (as translated into the effects of the behavior it predisposes in its bearer) to whether itself or instead other individual genes of its kind in the organism's relatives get replicated. The theory of kin selection substantiates this point.[6] Genes are "altruistic" as individuals but "selfish" with regard to their own kind. The policy statement that describes the behavioral disposition a gene directs is a selfish one if, like Wilson, we mean by a gene a <u>kind</u> of gene, a gene-type and not an individual gene.

The gene, <u>qua</u> gene-type, I call a super individual. It is a kind whose members share a community of purpose aimed impartially at the good of any and all members of the kind. The notion is easy to see if I first make up a human example. Suppose honest persons impartially aim at benefitting anyone who is honest, and no one else. Thus each honest person has a Kantian, impartial policy. If we could think of the assemblage of honest individuals as a super individual, what kind of policy would that super individual have? It aims at benefitting each and every member of the class that makes it up, and if we assume there is no composition fallacy involved in going from what benefits each and every honest person to what benefits the assemblage, then the super individual aims at benefitting itself. The super individual, unlike an individual honest person, cannot aim at the good of anything besides itself because we define it as the assemblage of persons who aim at benefitting persons like themselves. Any intentional beneficiary of an honest person is, by stipulation, part of the super individual.

Gene types and ant colonies are much more plausible candidates for super individuals. But the argument is the same. Each individual gene causes bodily structures or behavior that "aims" at the good (the perpetuation) of any gene of its type: When it can, an animal acts so as to favor the replication of genes in its relatives as well as in itself, and sometimes it does so at the expense of itself. In doing so the individual animal as well as the individual genes in the animal follow impartial policies. But if the super individual is defined as a class of similar genes (the gene-type) that impartially aim at benefitting each other and only each other, the policy of this super individual will be a selfish policy (assuming, again, that the case at hand allows us to go from what is distributively beneficial to what is collectively beneficial).

Think once more of Kant's kingdom of ends or community of rational beings. It is assumed that in the kingdom of ends an individual's inclination to benefit himself does not get in the way of rational law-like judgment, in other words, he follows the categorical imperative. As we saw, in this case each rational being treats every rational being including itself as an end and never a means but may treat nonrational beings as mere means. If we think of the community (the tribe, the colony) of rational beings as a super individual with a policy, that policy will be a selfish one: The policy of Kant's colony-individual is to benefit itself, and it necessarily benefits only itself because any beneficiary is a rational being and therefore by definition part of the super individual.

This is how, finally, we can find genuine selfishness in inanimate nature and lower organisms: super individuals have egoistic (selfish) policies. We can conclude that genes are selfish from one point of view and altruistic from another. Altruistic individual genes of a given kind will be group egoists if the behavior they cause aims at the good of their kind. Group egoism characterizes tribal morality from the point of view of the individuals who comprise the tribe, as we saw earlier. But in this section I want to discuss tribal morality from the point of view of the tribe and its relation to the individuals in it. The tribal moralist's tribe is usefully understood as a selfish super individual. Kant's kingdom of ends is a good example of one.

Entomologists have talked about ant and termite colonies as super individuals: The individual organism is the colony and the ants that make it up are its parts, they merely being more loosely connected physically with one another than are the parts of a person of the parts of an individual ant. The conception of a super individual appeals to entomologists because the various castes of ants in the colony altruistically perform specialized roles which serve the good of the colony much as in a person the various organs and cellular structures serve the good of the person.[7]

So we might offer the same kind of argument that was given in the case of genes: We do not find pure altruism from organisms in the ant-world without making an assumption about what is the organism and what are its parts. If the ant colony is the organism then we can say that it evolved to be completely selfish and is served by its parts, the ants, which evolved to serve selflessly. If the organisms are individual ants they follow impartial policies, but in doing so are group egoists--perfect patriots, we might say--with regard to their colony.

We can think of a person as a colony or super individual, like an ant heap. Or, more interestingly, we can think of individual persons as being related to society in the way in which individual ants are related to the ant colony, so that the society is the organism and particular persons are its parts. Politically repellant though it is, the latter model offers an illuminating view of some aspects of human social morality. As in the case of genes and ants, human group egoism can be thought of as the actions of the parts of a super individual for the super individual's own good, i.e., for the family's own good, the country's own good, or the species' own good. The idea may help to illuminate something otherwise puzzling: the apparent egoism and self-interest of persons who say "My family, my country (and so on) first," and who nonetheless are, contrary to self-interest, willing to sacrifice themselves for their family or their country. These are people who act like the genes and ants described above (and the members of Kant's kingdom of ends too, we might add): They are "selfish" regarding the good of their own kind, and altruistic as individuals.

Whether a policy is egoistic or altruistic depends on the concept of an individual we adopt. An organism's altruistic policy can simultaneously be aimed selfishly at the good of its kind; and calling the policy selfish, as seems natural in the case of genes, ants, and perhaps members of a fanatical army, seems to presuppose a different actor, a larger self that is actually selfish, a super individual of which the particular ants and soldiers function as parts or members. Exploring these notions beyond their programmatic presentation here might provide insights into individualist as contrasted with collectivist, organic elements of political thought; and we might acquire a better understanding of the conflicts between a person's "impartial morality," on the one hand, and his nested (and competing) loyalties.

Could non-conscious robots be racists, patriots, or speciesists? Compare the robot policy, "Only preserve robots of your own color" with the human policy, "Only preserve people of your own color." One might think that surely a robot, like a person, can find out what color it is and then preserve only those with similar colors. But if, as we have seen, robot Rl cannot learn "Oil thyself" without translating it into a universal policy, neither can it learn "Preserve robots of thine own color" without translating it into a universal policy. The argument is the same. To produce a robot analogue of racism we would simply program Rl to preserve white robots, Rl being a white one. But of course it would not matter in the slightest to Rl that it was white; it might perceive itself to be white, but only in the sense of discovering one more white robot to add to a list of robots to preserve. A person whose policy it is always to put white people

117

first, but absolutely independently of the fact that white is his own color, would be a strange racist indeed. If we count him a racist at all, he is a disinterested racist: the color would be morally or aesthetically valuable to him, it would be an ideal and not a loyalty.

The concept of the self as a particular is as necessary for loyalties as for egoism. The idea of prizing America, or anything, higher than something else just because it is one's own depends on possessing a concept of the self as a particular. Otherwise, the "just because" will be unintelligible. I, a person, have a concept of the self; other things and persons can be unique objects of value to me not because <u>they</u> are unique, but because from the standpoint of my consciousness I am unique. Just as an egoist puts himself first regardless of the exactly similar circumstances of his cloned replica, a loyalist puts his country, species, and so on, first, regardless of the similar circumstances of competing countries or species. It follows that non-conscious entities no more can be patriots or racists, in the sense of having loyalties rather than ideals, than they can be selfish. I said earlier that individual genes and ants can be thought of as perfect patriots with regard to the good of their kind. Now it should be clear they are "impartial patriots," following ideals rather than loyalties.

One thing I have been trying to explain is why people are so torn between altruism and selfishness. They often do not even know whether an action is selfish or altruistic, as when someone sacrifices himself for his career, his child, or his country. I suspect that the way we evolved is partly responsible for this. A person, being conscious, can aim at the good of a particular, himself; we call this selfishness. His genes, being non-conscious and therefore perfect Kantians, aim impartially at the good of their kind, which is dispersed within the person and his relatives; according to sociobiologists this prompts self-sacrificial behavior on the part of the person for the benefit of his relatives. Of course, what does the "aiming at" in each case is the person together with his genetic endowment. A person's genes help motivate him to act for the good of an individual (himself), while other genes in him help motivate him to act for the good of a super individual, namely the assemblage of relatives through which his kind of genes are spread. At least, this is how it is if the theory of kin selection is correct. And if it is, one evolutionary product (or byproduct) called consciousness prompts attitudes and judgments that are incompatible with the promptings of another evolutionary product, namely, our hereditary predispositions to certain kinds of self-sacrificial altruism.

Chapter IV: NOTES

1. Gilbert Harman, THE NATURE OF MORALITY (New York: Oxford University Press, 1977), Chapter 8.

2. Richard Hare, FREEDOM AND REASON (New York: Oxford University Press, 1963), Chapter 6.

3. Op. cit., Chapter 9.

4. Thomas Henry Huxley, "Evolution and Ethics," The Romanes Lecture, 1893.

5. Edward O. Wilson, SOCIOBIOLOGY: THE NEW SYNTHESIS (Cambridge: Harvard University Press, 1975), Chapter 1.

6. Kin selection is explained in W. D. Hamilton's classic paper "The Genetical Evolution of Social Behavior I, II," JOURNAL OF THEORETICAL BIOLOGY, 7 (1964), pp. 1-52. This paper worked out how self-sacrificial behavior on the part of individual organisms can be selected for in evolution. It will be briefly outlined in Section 6.3 For a summary see also Wilson's SOCIOBIOLOGY, or A. Oldenquist, "Evolution and Ethics," THE PERSONALIST, 59 (1978), pp. 58-69.

7. Darwin himself, in THE ORIGIN OF SPECIES, said that the extreme altruism found among the social insects posed the greatest single problem for the theory of natural selection. It was not until the work of W. D. Hamilton that the solution was worked out in any detail, although others, including Darwin and J.B.S. Haldane, hinted at it earlier.

V. REASONING WITHIN LIMITS

1.1 <u>Validity, Rules, and Consequences.</u> This discussion of moral reasoning ultimately will focus on a crucial and influential claim I call "the unanimity thesis"; it says that if people agree about the facts they will agree about morals. There are, however, two preliminary issues to consider which are related to reason giving. One concerns my disregard of the venerable distinction between judging actions by appealing to rules and judging actions by appealing to consequences. The other is the matter of explaining how there can be valid moral arguments if moral beliefs are dispositions like love and hate and moral judgments expressions of them. It was, of course, a common criticism that emotivism could not allow for logical relations among moral sentences.

On the one hand, it appears indubitable that the following argument is valid: "All thefts are wrong, A is a theft, therefore A is wrong." On the other hand, it seems that we cannot have validity without truth: In a valid deductive argument the conjunction of the premises together with the denial of the conclusion is a contradiction; and we understand a contradiction to be comprised of two contradictories, one true and one false. Does this mean there cannot be valid moral arguments unless the premises and conclusions are moral truths and falsehoods? Does the validity of moral arguments imply there are moral facts?

In Chapter Two I argued that while it is not very important whether moral judgments can be true or false, nonetheless the theory I defend allows it. One might worry that this implies it is unimportant whether moral arguments can be valid, or that they can be valid only in odd or honorific senses of the word. Consequently I want to show how there can be valid moral arguments even if there is no sense at all in which moral judgments are true or false. I will offer a theory that explains the validity of a moral argument in terms of the validity of some other, intimately related argument.

The following is analogous to what I have in mind. Suppose someone said that the argument form, "P Q, P, .'. Q" is not valid because the conjunction of "P Q, P" and "not Q" is not false, the reason being that statement variables lack truth values. Nevertheless we understand perfectly well what it means to call an argument form valid: It is valid in the sense that actual arguments with that form are valid. A valid argument form has instances, valid in virtue of the form, whose premises and conclusions have truth values. On my analogous explanation deductive moral arguments are like argument forms; hence I need to find other arguments that are their "instances" and which I can pair in a natural and obvious way with moral arguments. What is needed is an argument comprised of statements about the speaker's beliefs, a subjective analogue of the moral argument.

When a deductive argument is valid there is some impossible state of affairs that is represented by the premises together with the denial of the conclusion. For example, "All men being mortal, Socrates' being a man, and Socrates' not being mortal." Only if there are moral states of affairs can we claim there is an impossible one represented by "All abortions being immoral, X being an abortion, and X not being immoral," and on my theory there aren't any. Hence I need a literally impossible state of affairs to pair with

(1) All abortions are immoral, X is a case of abortion, and X is not immoral.

I suggest the following.

(2) Harry believes all abortions are immoral, X is a case of abortion, and Harry does not believe X is immoral.

It might be thought that (2) is not a contradiction because Harry may not believe that X is an abortion--he may never have heard of case X. But to think this is to neglect a general consequence of the denial of moral facts. A belief sentence usually is two propositions, "H believes that P," and "P" which is embedded in the former; this fact about belief sentences makes certain inferences defective that are not defective with other kinds of sentences. For example, if H believes all theft is hated, we cannot infer he believes theft X is hated because he may not know X is a theft. But if H hates all thefts, we can infer he hates theft X. However, if any nondescriptivist ethical theory is true, "H believes that P" (where P is "X is immoral") does not contain an embedded proposition. "H believes that X is immoral" is a unitary proposition and cannot be broken up into a main one and an embedded one. On my theory it means, "H is opposed to X." If, as the emotivists claimed, uttering "X is immoral" just expresses the speaker's attitude, or as the imperativists claimed is a disguised imperative, then the "Harry believes" in "Harry believes that abortion is immoral" does not intend a propositional object. The result, odd as it may seem, is that "Harry believes all abortions are immoral," when interpreted to mean "Harry is opposed to all abortions," is inconsistent with "X is an abortion and Harry does not think X is immoral." We can conclude, in accord with the theory, that "Harry believes all abortions are immoral, X is a case of abortion, and Harry does not believe X is immoral," is a contradiction: It says something inconsistent about Harry's dispositions.

Harry can, of course, _say_ that all abortion is immoral and abortion X is not immoral; he even can believe he holds both of these moral beliefs. But it can no more be true that he actually holds both than it can that he simultaneously is opposed and not opposed to all abortions. A plausible and interesting consequence is that a person can be mistaken about his own moral beliefs: He can think he morally opposes all so-and-sos, or some particular one, when in fact he does not; he is mistaken about his dispositions. It is a consequence of the theory that a person is simply unable to have contradictory moral beliefs. Moral beliefs are kinds of states of affairs and are not, in addition, propositional items, and we know there cannot exist contradictory states of affairs. But it does not follow that he cannot contradict himself, that is, say what is self-contradictory, for I have just finished defining the sense in which he can do this.

The theory makes the following non-normative argument valid:

> (3) Harry believes all killing is wrong, running over George is a killing, therefore Harry believes running over George is wrong.

Argument (3) corresponds to the first-person moral argument,

> (4) All killing is wrong, running over George is a killing, therefore running over George is wrong (said by Harry)

in the sense that we can map (4) onto (3): The minor premises are identical and argument (3) asserts that Harry actually has the moral beliefs he expresses in (4). Consequently, given any person's utterance of (4) we have a procedure for deriving a corresponding nonmoral argument (3). And now I can claim (4) is valid just in case corresponding (3) is valid, even though the sentences in (4), like the sentences in an argument form, may be neither true nor false. In a sense, "Harry believes killing is wrong" and Harry's act of saying "killing is wrong" are about the same thing: The judgment putatively manifests a disposition and the report asserts the presence of the disposition.

I am well aware that people seldom mean that all A's are wrong when they accept the rule "thou shalt not do A." My theory of moral belief is particularly amenable to more flexible accounts of general moral beliefs, since saying that someone is disposed to oppose A's can mean that he tends to oppose A's; or it can mean that he will oppose any particular A unless, under a different description, he at the same time more strongly favors it. Nonetheless, the interpretation "H is opposed to all A's," unusual though it may be, is needed as part of a theory of how deductive moral arguments can be valid. However slight one may think the role of deductive argument in moral reasoning, it nevertheless is important to show the possibility of such arguments.

124

Turning to what, at first sight at least, concerns the content instead of the form of moral reasoning, David Ross has remarked on a "clear antithesis" between ethical systems in which duty is the central theme, and those in which goods or ends are central.[1] It is an antithesis between deontologists who opt for "right," "ought," and "duty," and teleologists who opt for "good" and "value" as the fundamental terms of moral appraisal. The deontologists do battle with the teleologists and dispute, for example, whether "right" can be defined in terms of "good." I want to show that the deontologoical/teleological distinction is a false dualism; it does not mark fundamentally different theories about the ground of right and wrong but merely offers alternative ways of saying the same thing. My point of attack is to examine the distinction between actions and the consequences of actions, with an eye to discovering why some events or features count as parts of actions and others count as consequences.

How can we separate an action from its consequences with enough clarity and finality to support the deontological/teleological distinction? Most descriptions of what a person did refer to features that we could, if we wished, reclassify as consequences of simpler actions. Suppose someone is campaigning for Pasquarello. I might say, like a witness under cross-examination, that what he "actually" did was distribute posters, persuade Democrats to register, and the like, and that his being a campaigner is a consequence of this activity. And if I am asked what he actually did in distributing posters, I might reply that he went to the printers, picked up the posters, walked into all the local Democratic headquarters in the city, and so on; and that a consequence of these actions was that posters got distributed. This line can be pursued until all he "actually does" are what, by themselves, are morally insignificant basic actions.

Redescription goes equally well in the other direction: Ends or consequences can be redescribed as possible actions. Usage is flexible enough that it often is a matter of indifference whether we say a person did X, or did something else that had X as a consequence. We should be wary, however, of the intentional breaking down of actions for the purpose of mitigating responsibility: "You ruined his career."--"No I didn't, I merely told the truth." There is a bit of sophistry in this response, for while it can be a way of claiming that he did not ruin a career on purpose, it is fallacious to let the issue of responsibility hang on the classification, rather than the other way around, and suggest that a person somehow is less responsible for something if it gets classified as a consequence than if it gets classified as an action.

When a person does something, he causally initiates a sequence of events extending indefinitely into the future. Tied in various ways to the events are action descriptions and consequence descriptions, an indefinitely large series of them. I shall call these action descriptions and consequence descriptions by the neutral term "action/consequence components," or components for short. The components comprise a series, some of them prior to others, because the events to which they are tied comprise a causal sequence. A simplified series of action-consequence components is as follows:

Foot presses brake	car stops	accident avoided	mafia chief in other car saved

$C1\dots\dots\dots C2\dots\dots\dots C3\dots\dots\dots\dots C4\dots\dots Cn$

Some components of a series are simultaneous, some but not all are causally connected, and it is not altogether clear where a series begins or even where it ends. Now, which components should we include in the description of someone's action and which components should we include in the description of the consequences of his action? What seems clear is that there are many ways of dividing the series into action and consequences:

1. Harry trod on the brake / with the consequence that the car stopped.

2. Harry stopped the car / with the consequence that an accident was avoided.

3. Harry avoided the accident / with the consequence that the Mafia chief was saved.

4. Harry saved the life of the Mafia chief / with consequences X, Y, Z.

One and the same event or set of events can be associated with multiple action descriptions, for example, "pointing," "signaling," "feeling the air flow," where whether or not a description fits depends not only on what events occur but also on the intention of the agent or the applicability of a convention. For this reason actions and consequences are not just events: Action components can be "biting" or "signaling," and consequence components can be "a bite" or "a signal." When components C and C' of a single series are simultaneous, we often can say either that S did C with the consequence C' or that S did C' by doing C, even though C is not a cause of C'.

In particular cases there naturally are reasons why we refer to C as a result instead of an action (and vice versa). If C was unforeseen by the agent we often call it a consequence rather than something he did. We often call C a consequence if it was expected but not specifically intended. Yet some components are called "actions" rather than "results" even though they are unexpected and unintended, for example, when they are striking, unusual, important, harmful, or especially beneficial. Thus vehicular homicides and the accidental discovery of X-rays are things that were done, not merely results of other doings. But neither do we say that all intended components of a series are actions. When the process of bringing something about is complex and uncertain, the causal chains extending far into the future, we are inclined to say that a person has an aim, goal or end, the attainment of which will be a consequence of certain prior actions.

Yet to say there are grounds that incline us to call this sort of component an action and that sort a consequence is not to say that we must call them so, or that we invariably misuse language if we do not. Our sense for the right word is embodied in loose criteria, of the sort described above, that are frequently weak and easily defeatable. Our ability to shift the status of morally relevant components back and forth between "consequence" and "component of an action" solves one of the easier problems in Kant's ethics, namely that of justifying actions such as beneficial lies without appealing to consequences. One only needs to see that Kant did not allow his maxims, and consequently his conception of a kind of action, to be sufficiently complex: Is not a life-saving lie a kind of action? Consequences that justify are easily viewed as part of a more complex action.

The argument now can be laid out. Suppose Harry initiates a series of action/consequence components and we believe his act is wrong only in virtue of component C, everything else in the series being perfectly innocent. In most cases, we can correctly say either that Harry did action C, or that Harry did action B with consequence C. It is by itself of no moral significance whether we let C characterize the action or instead count it as a consequence of a simpler action B, for by hypothesis the only thing wrong-making is the nature of C. Consequently, if we believe B is wrong because it violates the principle, "Actions with C-type consequences are wrong," it would be irrational to deny C is wrong because it violates the rule, "C-type actions are wrong." And conversely, if C is wrong because it violates the rule, B is wrong because it violates the principle. If we are free to construe components as either specifications of the action or as consequences, then we are free to say either that the person did what was wrong because of certain consequences, or that he did what was wrong because his action was of a certain sort. And this means we may appeal to rules or consequences, as we please.

In FIVE TYPES OF ETHICAL THEORY C. D. Broad defined deontological and teleologoical ethical theories as follows:

Deontological theories hold that there are ethical propositions of the form: "Such and such a kind of action would always be right (or wrong) in such and such circumstances, no matter what its consequences might be." ... Teleological theories hold that the rightness or wrongness of an action is always determined by its tendency to produce certain consequences which are intrinsically good or bad.[2]

One problem with these definitions is that there isn't much difference between circumstances and consequences. Circumstances usually alter the outcome of actions, and often are taken to be the altered outcomes of actions. For example, Broad's deontologist might say lying is right in wartime circumstances where one needs to deceive the enemy, and "no matter what its consequences."

Definitions such as Broad's are empty because all the components deemed morally relevant by a deontologist are incorporated in the rule and in the specification of circumstances. In classifying these same components as consequences, the teleologist may claim he has an "external ground" for the morality of an action. He may think this shows that teleological justifications provide reasons and deontological justifications do not: The teleologist claims that an act is wrong because of some additional fact about it, namely its bad consequences, whereas the formalist merely proclaims that a kind of action is wrong.

We have seen, however, that there is no additional fact, there is just a game with words. The morally relevant components are distinct from the action they are taken to justify only because some philosopher who is a teleologist makes them so by dubbing them "consequences." A deontologist who takes the same components to be "wrong-making" will simply incorporate them into a more complex action description. There are no moral grounds for favoring the one classification over the other; sometimes there are slight grounds of usage. But the occasions on which our sense for the right word favors the teleologist probably are balanced by the occasions on which it favors the deontologist.

Not everything is classifiable either way: What about basic actions and irreducible consequences? Basic actions such as finger movements cannot be redescribed as consequences of simpler actions; remote and unintended consequences cannot, without stretching our sense for the right word too far, be redescribed as actions. When we reach activities simple enough, such as depressing a pedal, we cannot easily redescribe them as ends because we cannot easily think of antecedent actions that would lead to them. So we cannot help but use the language of rules and say "You ought to step on the brake." But we do have a choice about the effects of stepping on the brake. Only when we can separate the thing to be done from how it is done can we let the former be a goal and the latter rules for attaining it.

Because actions are irreducible, so too are rules. But principles are equally irreducible because some consequence-descriptions cannot be reformulated as action descriptions. Hence my reclassifiability thesis requires qualification in these two ways. The limits can be illustrated as follows:

Nerve message sent to foot	Harry pushes on brake	The car stops (or: H. stops car	Mafia chief saved (or: H. saves Mafia chief)	Mafia chief has grand-child named Harry
C1	C2	C3	C5	Cn
Neural process, not an action	Basic action	Describable as act or consequences		Irreducible consequence

Nevertheless, actions claimed to be obligations are usually nonbasic and rather more complex than finger movements. Actions may be irreducible, at one end of a series of act/consequence components, and consequences may be irreducible, at the other end, but the arena of moral judgment lies mostly between these extremes.

5.2 <u>The Unanimity Thesis.</u> Normative beliefs come in different strengths for different people. Harry and Max may agree that hunting is wrong, that fire-bombing cities in wartime is unjustified, that political bribery is unethical, but differ in the intensity with which they hold these beliefs. On the proposed theory the phenomenon is easily explained: Harry and Max are each opposed to X, only

Harry is more strongly opposed than Max and the measure of the relative strength of his opposition lies in the behavior he emits. All of our normative beliefs have some degree of importance for us and it is doubtful that any two people who agree about an issue hold their beliefs with exactly the same strength or fervor. They may give exactly the same reasons but one may feel more strongly about the matter than the other. Neither should we be surprised if a person condemns X less strongly today than he did five years ago, even though his reasons are the same today as they were five years ago.

The measure of how strongly we are opposed to something lies in the comparative judgments we are prepared to make. Many moral disputes arise because one person feels more strongly about the issue than another and not because they have conflicting principles or incompatible nonmoral beliefs. If we agree that N is bad but I think it is worse than you do, then I (but not you) may say it is worse than M, I alone may think that retaliation is justified, or I alone may be willing to sacrifice A to get rid of N.

The ubiquitousness of moral and evaluative disagreements that do not turn on issues of fact or principle should be obvious: We agree X is very expensive but I say it is too expensive. We agree that the suspect's sudden hand movement is ominous and warrants some response, but I think it justifies the officer's shooting him and you do not. We agree about the probable gains and losses of dropping atomic bombs on Japan in World War II, but you think the gains outweigh the losses and I do not. Philosophers largely ignore this source of moral disagreement, probably because the standard explanations available will not account for it. Most assume that if Harry lets reason A outweigh reason B, and Max does not, there must be some additional matter they disagree about: if not the facts, then some third reason or principle, C, that Harry accepts and Max rejects. But this isn't necessarily the case.

I now want to consider an example at length; I want to probe and worry it in the attempt to discover something about the origin and avoidability of moral diversity. Suppose Harry believes it was wrong to fire-bomb German cities in World War II and

Max believes it was justified. Harry says, "Fire-bombing was wrong because it was the mass killing of civilians"; Max says, "Fire bombing German cities was justified because it was likely to bring victory sooner." Why do they disagree over whether slightly shortening the war justified the mass killing of civilians? Numerous attitudes and factual beliefs could account for it, but I shall suppose them to agree about all of these save one: the degree of wickedness they attribute to the Nazis. They agree, for example, that foreigners' lives count as much as others, that the effects of fire-bombing cities are so-and-so, what the Nazis did and planned to do was such-and-such. However, Max believes the Nazis were evil enough to justify fire-bombing their cities and Harry does not.

Something's being "evil enough" to justify so-and-so isn't always another piece of information. It is not that Max gives the Nazis a 10 and Harry gives them an 8 on a wickedness scale. We learn how wicked Max thinks the Nazis are from the price he is willing to see paid to thwart them and from the comparative judgments he makes. When he says, "The Nazis' actions are evil enough to justify fire-bombing," we should not ask, "Oh? And how evil is that?" If he answers, "Worse than Ghengis Khan and not as bad as Stalin," he tells us something, but not much; he gives us a relative scale. Often the only answer is no answer: "Fire-bombing is justi-fied; that's how evil."

Suppose that whereas Harry and Max each describe living under Nazi occupation in the same way, Harry learned his facts from books and Max actually lived in Nazi occupied France. So Harry and Max have had different experiences; Harry has never met a Nazi. Max has seen hostages shot and watched the struggles of a young woman being carried off by the Gestapo; Harry has read about some of these, has been told about the others by Max, and believes they occurred. Neither of them has a reason based on the facts and logic of the case that the other does not acknowl-edge. Since I am supposing they share all the beliefs they take to be relevant to how evil the Nazis were, their different experiences are probable causes of their moral disagreement.

It is not that Max could not have reasons; he might be a virtuoso of casuistry and construct reasons which to him justify fire-bombing if it decreases the "most probable duration" of the war by N days or more. But few people have this virtuosity and I am supposing Max does not. What Max says is, "I have lived under those beasts and you have not; I approve any measure which...," etc. If there are real cases like this, and I submit there are, some moral disagreements are intractable not because Harry and Max disagree about a matter of fact or principle but because they disagree about the degree of wickedness of the Nazis: One of them is more strongly opposed than is the other.

In the light of this what should we say about the well-known claim that if everyone who met certain conditions of mental heath, rationality, etc., had the same factual beliefs then they would have the same moral beliefs? It is crucial for certain kinds of ethical theories and I shall call it "the unanimity thesis." The universalizability principle required a person to judge similar cases similarly; the unanimity thesis extends this requirement across persons. I will try to show that it is incorrect largely because it applies across persons: Our basic moral beliefs and, in particular, the degrees of intensity with which they are held are caused by our genes and our experiences; hence two equally rational people might agree completely about what the relevant facts are and yet disagree morally because these causes are different. The conclusion I will reach is that any plausible defense of the unanimity thesis turns it into a causal claim rather than a claim about reasons, in particular the claim that similar causal antecedents produce similar moral beliefs.

The importance of the unanimity thesis is this. Most of us believe that in the realm of what we see and hear around us, normal rational people who undertake similar observations will make similar reports. We believe this because we have observed it to be so and because we believe there are physical facts that determine what a rational, competent, informed and healthy observer will observe. We believe there exist facts that are relevant to what we see and hear, that there is some determinate reality for normal perceivers to perceive.

Now, if ideal <u>moral</u> observers agree, it does not follow that there are moral facts about which they agree; for there could be other reasons why they agree, such as similar genetically determined desires and emotions, or similar experiences, or both. But if ideal moral observers do not agree, in other words if the unanimity thesis is false, it seems to follow that there are no moral facts and therefore ethics is not like perception in this respect. For if there were moral facts, would not the moral judgments of different people be alike if these people shared whatever was relevant to perceiving a moral fact? Will not equal perceivers perceive alike if there is something external to perceive? Hence the unanimity thesis seems to be a necessary (but not a sufficient) condition for any theory of moral facts and it behooves the moral objectivist to defend it. Moral objectivists in fact do defend the unanimity thesis, even if they think moral objectivism does not strictly imply it. Philosophers' commitment to the unanimity thesis is a quaint testimonial to their faith in a uniform human nature even though, in other contexts, many of the same philosophers do not believe in human nature.

It is safe to say that no two people have had exactly similar experiences. Even if Harry and Max live in the same French town under Nazi occupation they will see and experience different things. And each may see the same thing and be affected differently. Different reactions or intensities of reaction may be triggered by other experiences they have had, for example, a young woman they see beaten and led away may be beautiful to Max but not to Harry, or she may attempt to ward off blows with the kinds of movements his sister used as a child. It is plausible to suppose that Max's unique experiences partly cause how evil he thinks the Nazis are, and hence partly cause what measures against them he thinks are justified. Moreover, if what we suffer and enjoy can affect the strength of our moral beliefs, we must admit these can include childhood and infantile experiences we have forgotten. This would be evidence that experiences themselves, not just the beliefs they produce, influence moral belief. Factual beliefs we have forgotten or repressed cannot enter into an account of moral disagreement that is based on disagreement about the facts.

Our moral and evaluative beliefs also depend on feelings and emotions, and these in turn depend on something more than just factual beliefs. The unanimity thesis ignores some of the emotional determinants of our values. A person brought up in a world without love, or in an environment of fear, hostility, repression, or physical and economic hardship, is likely to have different values (and value intensities) from those of someone brought up in opposite surroundings.

Finally, the nature and strength of our prevailing feelings depend not only on experiences but also on inherited peculiarities of body chemistry. This is a topic that will be pursued further in the next chapter. Even if Harry and Max had exactly similar nonmoral beliefs and experiences, but had different genetically determined body chemistries and hence somewhat different prevailing emotions and feelings, it is still plausible to claim that, because of this, they have different intensities of moral beliefs about the Nazis. Edward O. Wilson and other sociobiologists have argued that there are important genetic causes of moral attitudes. Wilson says,

> The biologist, who is concerned with questions of physiology and evolutionary history, realizes that self-knowledge is constrained and shaped by the emotional control centers in the hypothalamus and limbic system of the brain. These centers flood our consciousness with all the emotions--hate, love, guilt, fear, and others--that are consulted by ethical philosophers who wish to intuit the standards of good and evil. What, we are then compelled to ask, made the hypothalamus and limbic system? They evolved by natural selection. That simple biological statement must be pursued to explain ethics and ethical philosophers...at all depths.[3]

135

This is hyperbole and a scientist's artless arrogance; I have my doubts that evolutionary history (or anything for that matter) can explain ethical philosophers at all depths. But it is highly probable that genetically determined characteristics partly mold a person's moral and evaluative beliefs and that these characteristics vary from individual to individual. At present, neurochemists have only sketchy knowledge of the enzymes produced in our brains, but it is almost certain that individual variation in the production of these enzymes is partly hereditary and that a person's prevailing feelings and emotions are influenced by the levels at which they are produced. Certainly no one knows the proportionate inputs of "nature" and "nurture," of genetically determined enzyme production and environment. But it is clear there is considerable individual variation in sexual desires, optimism or pessimism, depression, suspicion, or trust, acceptance or rejection of one's lot, capacity to love, and so on.

Feelings, emotions, fears, and desires that are in large part hereditary are principle causes of our basic moral beliefs and their varying intensities; and these are causes that vary from person to person. We cannot look upon the brain as a black box or mere intervening variable when we speculate about the causes of moral beliefs. If morals are caused by experience and emotional makeup, and if the latter depend on enzymes secreted by our ancient, tribal brains, heredity as well as experience cause individual variation in their nature and intensity. The plausibility of the unanimity thesis varies inversely with the plausibility of this causal hypothesis.

A supporter of the unanimity thesis can respond to this. Max, who has lived under the Nazis, has many beliefs Harry lacks, for example, about the details of the expression on the face of the girl he saw led away by the Gestapo. Because two people never have exactly similar experiences they never have exactly similar factual beliefs: They at least have different memory beliefs. A _fortiori_, we never have a case of moral disagreement and complete factual agreement. True, their different factual beliefs do not necessarily conflict; nonetheless the difference might explain their moral disagreement.

So one can still claim that were Harry to share all of Max's factual beliefs he would agree with him about the morality of fire-bombing German cities. This move does not, of course, prove the unanimity thesis, but it does appear to eliminate counter-examples. Thus a moral intellectualist might argue that Harry and Max in fact do have different factual beliefs about the Nazis--the mental records of their different experiences--and that this difference explains their moral disagreement.

The rejoinder that first comes to mind is that the defender of the unanimity thesis somehow has lost sight of the difference between relevant and irrelevant facts. The issue, after all, is whether experience and heredity, which are mere causes, account for some moral disagreements between rational, informed people, or instead, that all disagreement is due to failure to satisfy certain idealizing conditions. Falling back on the claim that Harry and Max do not have <u>exactly</u> similar factual beliefs looks like a concession that factual beliefs might account for moral disagreement whether or not any rational person would accept them as reasons (and equally weighty reasons). But if they are not relevant as reasons they take their place alongside the experiences and hereditary factors I have argued can simply cause Harry and Max to disagree.

To openly seize upon the causal interpretation of the unanimity thesis is to fall back on a version of determinism: H and M's having exactly similar nonmoral beliefs causes them to have exactly similar moral beliefs. This hardly is ground for concluding that moral controversies are rationally decidable; cognitivist ethical theories, including ideal observer theories, gain nothing if they merely specify conditions that produce moral unanimity. What they require is not merely unanimity but unanimity that would result from the satisfaction of certain idealizing conditions alone, these being conditions that, on general epistemic grounds, are relevant to the acquisition of knowledge or, at least, to the acquisition of rational belief. In any case, however, this particular causal defense seems to be wrong.

137

One problem is that it is difficult to isolate the idea of A's relevance as a reason except in terms of our belief that if we consciously abandoned A we would abandon B. In general, we call a factual belief a reason if we think our moral belief depends on it. We need not independently discern its reasonhood or feel its relevance. We may just note that when the one belief is given up so is the other. This might be a matter of watching causation at work in oneself. It does not seem to be phenomenologically possible to precisely distinguish the notion, "relevant as a reason" from the notion, "relevant as a cause." It seems as difficult to isolate the idea of the moral relevance of a factual belief from the conviction that if I abandoned A I would abandon B, as it seemed, for David Hume, to isolate the notion of causal necessity from the ideas of constant conjunction, etc. Nevertheless, a factual belief on which a person discovers his moral belief depends usually will be accepted as a reason for it.

Once we begin to speak of causes we can see that factual beliefs are only one kind of potential cause of moral beliefs. I argued that two people with exactly similar factual beliefs might morally disagree because of genetic causes that affect their neurochemistry. They might disagree because of different past experiences whose memory traces are forgotten. Moreover, when we say two people share a belief we usually mean they accept the same written or spoken proposition. Harry and Max may each say sincerely, "The Dresden air raid in 1945 caused 100,000 deaths." They mean the same by their words and have the same belief, but what this belief means to each can be very different. Similar sincere sentences do not guarantee that the corresponding neurological and psychological conditions are similar, and these underlying conditions, when different, could account for the different influence the same factual belief has on different people. For these reasons, the unanimity thesis is a poor causal hypothesis if it only mentions beliefs, because it competes with the more comprehensive hypothesis that says experiences together with genetic make-up cause both moral beliefs and factual beliefs.

The argument against the unanimity thesis is assisted by a constraint on what can be a reason. Reasons are the sort of things one person can communicate to another, experiences are not. Reasons, after all, can enter into arguments with moral conclusions; their importance lies in the publicly accessible place they have in arguments. Therefore reasons cannot be ineffable. If Max says he has reasons why German cities should be fire-bombed that Harry can never have, i.e., ineffable reasons, then he is really talking about the role of his experiences in causing him to believe as he does. Experiences can be ineffable, but the relation an experience has to a moral belief, when it has any, is only causal.

This distinction is crucial for ever so many moral controversies. People often say things such as, "If you had been through what I have been through you wouldn't think it was wrong to throw him out" or, "Wait until you are beaten and robbed on the street by teenage toughs before you decide how the police should treat them." And they may add, "...so I have reasons you cannot have until you have been through what I have been through." We may be told exactly what he has been through and still not have his "reasons." The law and educated moral thinking rightly reject this notion of a reason. A moral community cannot admit the ineffable as a reason, although it can and does respond to generally shared experiences. It admits as reasons only what can be said in words, and then shared with the aid of imagination and empathy, against a background of common experiences. Yet who can deny that what cannot be shared can account for moral disagreement? The law wisely does not allow the victim of a crime to set the criminal's "just" penalty, and in prohibiting this admits that the victim's incommunicable experiences, as distinct from his communicable beliefs about his experiences, can determine what he believes is just punishment. In the case of Max and Harry, it is what Max cannot narrate to Harry, namely the brute experiences themselves, that most plausibly accounts for the greater intensity of his moral condemnation of Nazis.

5.3 Will the Ideal Observers Quarrel? A notorious objection to ideal observer theories is that

we have no guarantee that two ideal observers would
agree. I shall develop the objection as follows. A
theory that says M is a true moral judgment if and
only if an ideal observer would affirm M is self-
contradictory if it is even logically possible that
one ideal observer would affirm M and another would
affirm not M: For the theory would imply that "M"
and "not M" could both be true. The force of the
objection is that there is no way to show the logical impossibility of two ideal observers disagreeing; one would have to be able to deduce the
impossibility of disagreement from the statement of
the idealizing conditions which define an ideal
observer. And the reason why this cannot be done is
that the characteristics that define a true moral
judgment are not features of the object or act being
judged, but features of some possible being who must
then react or form an opinion. It does not help to
substitute "justified" or "rational" for "true." If
it is logically possible that two ideal observers
should disagree, then according to the theory it is
logically possible that both "M" and "not M" are
justified or rational.

There is another version of the ideal observer
theory, proposed by Roderick Firth, that might be
thought to escape the argument. Firth proposes that
we

> construe statements of the form "x is P," in
> which P is some particular ethical predi-
> cate, to be identical in meaning with state-
> ments of the form: "Any ideal observer would
> react to x in such and such a way under such
> and such conditions."[4]

Ideal observers, for Firth, are hypothetical beings,
which means, I guess, that one can postulate any
number of them. His view is that "X is P" is true
only if all possible ideal observers would react in
such-and-such a way to X.

Let us fill this out by saying,

(1) Theft T is morally permissible

means

 (2) Any ideal observer would react positively to T,

and

 (3) Theft T is not morally permissible

means

 (4) Any ideal observer would react negatively to T.

Suppose the IO's are split with the result that (2) and (4) are false. It follows at once that (1) and (3) are false, which is a contradiction. Moreover, if it is even logically possible that one IO reacts positively and one reacts negatively to A, it is logically possible that contradictories (1) and (3) are both false; and it certainly seems logically possible for them to react in this way. Whereas the first version of the theory had the consequence that "M" and "not M" could both be true, Firth's version appears to imply that "M" and "not M" could both be false. This is not an improvement.

Consider a different interpretation of Firth's theory according to which an IO can react only one way: If every IO would emit reaction R toward action A, A is permissible, otherwise not. Thus the theory now says that A is permissible if and only if all IO's would emit R toward A. What is wrong with this version is that it says A is not permissible in the logically possible case in which one IO emits R toward A and another does not. Why should we think A is not permissible if IO reaction is equally divided? The theory is now consistent but its criterion is arbitrary. More importantly, why should we honor the opinion or reactions of IO's at all in the logically possible case in which they bicker about what is moral just as we do? The fact is that ideal observer theories presuppose the unanimity thesis; they assume that IO's would never disagree and quarrel as we do.

The ideal observer theory is an incoherent hybrid of two incompatible theories, ethical relativism and what we might call objectivism or absolutism; it gets its appeal by falling back on each to counter the inadequacies of the other. Ethical relativism says there are moral truths, but these truths are relative to opinions or feelings. IO theories are relativistic because they affirm that A is wrong because IO's would respond in some way; they deny the converse, that IO's would respond in a certain way because A is wrong. When faced with the logical possibility of divided IO opinion, a relativist who admits he is a relativist would say, "A is right for IO X and A is wrong for IO Y." But we have no need for IO's in order to say this sort of thing.

To avoid the usual implications of relativism IO theories fall back on two assumptions that are plausible only if there are moral facts independent of the opinions of anyone including IO's. First, they assume the unanimity thesis, thus guaranteeing harmonoy in the ranks of the IO's. If there are moral facts that are logically independent of opinion, perfect knowers will not disagree about what they are. The assumption of IO unanimity is a safe one only if we do not define moral truth in terms of the reactions of IO's. If their reaction defines moral truth, we cannot prove they won't quarrel; if their reaction does not but merely tests for an already existing truth, we do not need them.

Second, IO theories assume that the idealizing conditions are epistemic criteria. The requirements of perfect observation, rationality, and sanity are, of course, taken from the ideal conditions for acquiring empirical knowledge. Otherwise there is no point in calling the observer ideal and the theory would be no better than one that said A is moral if any randomly selected creature scratches its ear. However, the very idea of an idealizing characteristic being an epistemic criterion is inconsistent with the claim that the reactions of IO's <u>define</u> moral truth. Epistemic criteria are criteria that yield knowledge when satisfied. What knowledge is an IO supposed to acquire in virtue of being omniscient, rational, and sane? Moral knowledge? But then its reactions cannot define it, unless we suppose the sole function of each IO's omniscience is to predict IO reactions, in which case the IO's sanity would come into question. If the epistemic criteria guide the IO to reaction R, then R is the correct reaction: the IO has hit on the truth. If this is so, theft is not wrong because the IO has reaction R, the IO has reaction R because theft is wrong. IO's are defined as entities that perfectly satisfy whatever conditions of knowledge there are, hence if there is anything to know they will know it. But the theory denies there is anything to know. There either is something to know, that is, moral knowledge, or there isn't. If there is, we do not need the concept of an IO except as a model of the perfect moral scientist; if there isn't, then the IO does not need knowledge, rationality, and sanity, except insofar as these are in general nice qualities to have.

Frank Chapman Sharp says the following in the course of explaining a version of the ideal observer theory:

> Now, knowledge is of two kinds; ... one is acquaintance with; the other, knowledge about. The former is given in immediate experience, whether in the world of sense or in the inner world of pleasure, pain, emotion, or desire.... If, then, a moral judgment is to be valid, it must be either a judgment based upon a complete acquaintance with the whole situation in all its relevant details or, since this is rarely or perhaps never attainable, such a judgment as would result from an acquaintance with the whole situation.[5]

In stressing acquaintance Sharp goes beyond merely claiming that an ideal observer must possess all the truths relevant to a moral situation. He wants to ensure that anyone who met the idealizing conditions would make the same moral judgment, and in insisting on knowledge by acquaintance Sharp suggests that if two IO's had the same experiences they would have the same moral beliefs. His view is plausible precisely because he comes closer to stating causal conditions which, if true of any two people, ensure their moral agreement; but he still leaves out childhood experiences and genetic causes.

The case against the unanimity thesis now can be completed. On the one hand, I argued that Harry and Max could accept a common list of propositions they think relevant to fire-bombing German cities and yet disagree about the morality of it. I concluded that what plausibly accounts for their moral disagreement are factors that do not count as reasons, such as Max's seeing the expression on the face of the girl dragged off by the Gestapo, and which affect the strength of his moral beliefs and, in turn, his comparative judgments. On the other hand, if we suppose Harry and Max to have had the same experiences and heredity we ensure moral unanimity; but we do so at the cost of making it a corollary of determinism. The satisfaction of epistemic idealizing conditions alone cannot plausibly be claimed to ensure unanimity. Saying two beings can be caused to have similar moral attitudes is no more a ground for claiming those attitudes are truths, or are rational, than is saying two beings can be caused to emit similar cries of pain or courtship behavior is a ground for claiming those bits of behavior are truths.

What is important for ethical theory is not unanimity but how one would achieve it. Suppose that everyone who satisfied certain idealizing conditions shouted "Boo!" or "Bravo!" at the ends of concerts in perfect agreement. This would give comfort (but not proof) to those who believed shouts of 'Boo!' and 'Bravo!' were ways of expressing aesthetic truths. But if instead we claim that everyone who has exactly similar past experiences emits similar responses at concerts, we replace the idealizing conditions with mere causes. Our new claim is on somewhat firmer ground because it says similar past experiences cause similar end-of-concert behavior. But what supported the claim that responses at concerts expressed aesthetic truths was the relevance the idealizing conditions were assumed to have to rationality and the attainment of knowledge. Unanimity by itself constitutes no evidence whatever for thinking that what we utter unanimously is true, or false, or either true or false. So too in the case of moral judgments: If we stick at similar idealizing conditions the unanimity thesis is almost certainly false. If we supplement them with similar causes, the moral unanimity that would result is irrelevant to whether or not those unanimous moral beliefs are true, or false, or neither true nor false.

Chapter V: NOTES

1. William David Ross, THE RIGHT AND THE GOOD (Oxford: The Clarendon Press, 1930), Ch. 1.

2. C. D. Broad, FIVE TYPES OF ETHICAL THEORY (London: Routledge and Kegan Paul, 1951), pp. 206-207.

3. Edward O. Wilson, SOCIOBIOLOGY: THE NEW SYNTHESIS (Cambridge: Harvard University Press, 1975), p. 3.

4. Roderick Firth, "Ethical Absolutism and the Ideal Observer" in W. Sellars and J. Hospers (eds.), READINGS IN ETHICAL THEORY, 2nd ed. (Englewood Cliffs: Prentice-Hall, 1970), pp. 200-221.

5. Frank Chapman Sharp, GOOD WILL AND ILL WILL (Chicago: The University of Chicago Press, 1950), Chapter 5.

VI. REASONS AND CAUSES

6.1 <u>Reasons and Causes.</u> Few people doubt that
moral beliefs have causes. We can point to the
relative uniformity of moral beliefs in uniform
environments, or to our conviction that "ultimate"
moral beliefs, by which I mean general moral beliefs
not supported by other moral beliefs, cannot come
from nothing. It is easy to suppose that one's
ultimate moral beliefs have causes because <u>ex
hypothesi</u> there are no reasons to get in the way of
a casual explanation. I wish to maintain, however,
that <u>all</u> of our moral and evaluative beliefs have
causes. This raises the question whether reasons
explanations and causal explanations compete with
one another. Suppose, for example, that Max believes
that abortion is immoral and gives the reason that
abortion is the taking of innocent human life; but
we believe the cause is his adolescent experiences
in a family strongly opposed to abortion. What then
shall we say about his reason? That it is irrelevant
and ornamental, pure rationalization, or what? In
this case we cannot claim that the reason is identical with the cause because they appear to be entirely different things: the one has to do with taking
human life and the other with the effects of his
relatives' shouting.

Do we commit the "genetic fallacy" if we think
that the cause and the reason can compete, since the
reason is about "P" and the cause is about "H
believes that P"? Is not Max's reason either good
or bad, regardless what causes him to believe what
he believes? But if moral beliefs are dispositions,
"H believes A is immoral" means something like, "H
is opposed to A" and does not contain an embedded
proposition. So how could the reason be about "P"
and the cause be about "H believes that P"? It
looks as though the reason and the cause pretend to
explain the same thing.

The view that will be developed is this: All
moral beliefs have environmental and genetic causes,

most of them have reasons, and the reason and the cause are always distinct. If a person is rationalizing, an explanation in terms of his reasons and a correct causal explanation compete in the sense that his reasons constitute an inadequate explanation of his belief and are "not the real reason" why he holds it. If a person is not rationalizing the reason and the cause do not compete but complement one another. In the latter case a person's reasons explain his moral belief in two ways: (a) They point the way to the causes of his moral belief; what I mean by "point the way" will emerge shortly. (b) Reasons explain a person's moral belief in virtue of being classificatory accounts; they tell us where someone is coming from regarding a moral opinion in the sense of telling us his principles and the factual beliefs that determined how he applied them.

I begin with a brief consideration of reasons for actions, which we shall see differ as much from reasons for factual beliefs as they do from reasons for moral beliefs. Suppose Adolph went to a movie and gives the reason that it was a Victor Mature movie and that Victor Mature is his favorite actor. However, we have good evidence he was caused to go by a hypnotic suggestion unrelated to Victor Mature. In this case we would deny that the reason he gives, however sincere, is "the real reason" why he went to the movie, on the grounds that it is a poorer explanation: It is more likely, we suppose, that he went because of the hypnosis than because it was a Victor Mature movie.

The reason he gives could have been the best explanation, in the absence of hypnosis. Or the "real reason" could have been another purpose: Adolph wanted to meet a certain girl and knew she would be at the movie. The real reason why he went was that he might bump into her at the movie, in the sense that he would not have gone did he not believe she would be there; this desire is what made him go. But Adolph does not know this is why he went; he thinks he went solely because it was a Victor Mature movie. We can conclude that his reason is simply incorrect.

148

When we are concerned with the explanation of an action we are not satisfied that the reason a person sincerely gives is the reason why he did it unless we are willing to rule out competing causes. Someone's reason can be incompatible with a straightforward causal explanation of the action. Thus Adolph's reason why he went to the movie is an incorrect account of why he went, given that he went because of a hypnotic suggestion, although it is a correct account of why he thought he went. This is not because purposive explanations are in general incompatible with causal explanations but because reasons for action are themselves a kind of causal explanation; the issue is whether a reason for acting is the correct causal explanation. (It may at the same time also be another kind of explanation, for example, a taxonomic one, but that does not concern us here.)

Some philosophers, for example, Charles Taylor and Norman Malcolm, have maintained that neurophysiological and other purely physical causes of a person's behavior necessarily compete with purposive explanations of the behavior.[1] I am arguing that this view is incorrect and that they only sometimes compete. The reason Adolph gives sometimes is a very plausible candidate for what made him go to the movie and sometimes it is a very implausible candidate for what made him go. The hypnotic suggestion and his reason can be unrelated, competing causal hypotheses for why he went, and only the former might be the correct one. On the other hand, and contrary to the Taylor-Malcolm view, causes can occur in chains and there is no obstacle to a reason and some neurophysiological or environmental cause both figuring in the same chain of causes. If my desire or purpose causes me to go to the movie, a set of brain processes cause the desire, and genetic and environmental factors cause the brain processes, the teleological and nonteleological elements of this chain are <u>all</u> causes of my going to the movie and do not in any way compete with one another.

Reasons for and causes of factual beliefs do not relate to each other as they do in the case of action. A causal account of a person's factual belief is not relevant to the correctness or cogency

149

of his reason for believing, whereas a causal account of an action can show his reason for acting to be simply false. A reason for a factual belief is a reason for its being <u>true</u>; but actions cannot be true. A factual belief is about something, actions are not. This is why the reasons for and causes of action are about the same thing and the reasons for and causes of a factual belief are about different things, i.e., P and a person's believing that P. In general the difference is between the explanation of some condition, disposition, or bit of behavior, and the explanation of the kind of thing that intends a propositional object. I have labored the difference because I want to show that moral reasons are in some ways like reasons for action and in some ways like reasons for factual beliefs.

If a moral belief is a disposition to oppose or support something, then, like an action but unlike a factual belief, it is non-propositional and does not point beyond itself. To assume that "why A is immoral" contrasts with "why Harry believes A is immoral" in the same way "why the house is vacant" contrasts with "why Harry believes the house is vacant" is to assume that moral beliefs are propositional. But moral reasons do not fit the action model either: They are not causes of anything, unlike reasons for action.

Reasons can be understood as linguistic items that enter into logical relations with other linguistic items: I can put my reasons in the form of an argument. On the other hand, we can also understand reasons as the corresponding beliefs and desires: Adolph's belief that the movie is a Victor Mature movie and whatever state of Adolph "Victor Mature is my favorite actor" expresses. In this sense reasons are nonlinguistic items and therefore do not assert or entail anything. In what follows I take moral reasons to be linguistic items and I call the corresponding psychological items "reason beliefs." It does not matter which way one does this; as long as one makes the correct moves thereafter everything will turn out the same whichever of these senses of "reason" one opts for.

Independent of this terminological issue is a substantive claim: Harry's believing that killing innocent human beings is immoral together with his believing that abortion is killing innocent human beings can be the cause of his believing abortion is immoral. Whether we label these elements reasons or reason beliefs, they can be links in a chain of causes whose effect is his believing abortion is immoral. Nevertheless, a person's reason beliefs are not always causes of his moral belief. As in the case of reasons for action, he does not believe A is immoral because of his reasons if instead something else, not causally related to his reason beliefs, makes him believe A is immoral. The ultimate causes of moral beliefs and of the degrees of strength with which we hold them--our experiences and genetic makeup--may or may not operate through our reason beliefs.

Suppose we wanted to know what causes Harry to believe that all A is C, when he believes that all A is B, all B is C, and if A is B and B is C then A is C. One answer is, "Harry's belief that all A is B, all B is C, and if A is B and B is C then A is C." This indeed is a cause, but boring and uninformative because it adds little or nothing, in addition to the reason he gives, to our understanding of why Harry believes all A is C. It merely gives a psychological account that parallels his logical inference and tells us that if someone believes an argument is sound he usually believes the conclusion. Similarly in the case of moral beliefs, one cause of Harry's belief that abortion is immoral may consist of his belief that killing innocent human beings is immoral, his belief that abortion is a case of that, and the inference belief. But we want to introduce causes at a deeper level.

Since causes can occur in chains, the cause of Harry's belief that A is immoral can be his experiences and heredity, and also his reason-beliefs: Everything on the chain is a cause. Hence; if Harry believes M because of his reasons (literally, because of his reason beliefs), this remains true even though his experiences and heredity cause him to believe M. We can pick out many items on a chain of causes and call almost any of them the cause of M as a way of spotlighting it, without implying either competing causes or over-determination. But if A and B are independent causes in the sense that, like a witch doctor's curse and a bacterium, they are on separate chains of causes, we can say that A and B might be either competing or overdeterminants. Whether or not he believes M because of his reasons depends on whether or not his reason-beliefs are part of the causal chain through which the cause operates. If his reason-beliefs are not part of this causal chain it is false that he believes M because of his reasons. In this case the reasons are indeed ornamental and constitute what in Section 6.2 I call a rationalization.

Thus my explanation of the relevance of both reasons and causes is that when Harry's moral belief is caused by his reason beliefs, he believes because of his reasons and also because of the environmental and genetic causes of his reason beliefs. For example, suppose I believe capital punishment ought to be abolished unless it is a better deterrent than life imprisonment and also believe it is not a better deterrent. That is my reason. What I hypothesize is a cause of my reason-beliefs when we reach that point, in tracing back my reasons, where they are not supported by further reasons I accept. One of these ultimate reasons might be that killing, legal or otherwise, is wrong unless there is a better contrary reason. I assume that what causes me to have these reason-beliefs also causes me to believe what I deduce from them. Given this, we can now claim that I believe that capital punishment is wrong because of my reasons, that it is on account of my reasons that I believe it, and that learning what my reasons are will lead a person to the causes of my moral belief. I have hypothesized a case in which my reasons are relevant to what makes me believe what I do about capital punishment, in the sense that the causes operate through my reason beliefs rather than independently of them.

Given the distinction made earlier between reasons and reason beliefs, the causes are not identical with my reasons. Neither do they in the above case compete with my reasons: They complement my reasons and work through the correlative reason beliefs. An intellectually satisfying explanation

of my moral belief requires both my reasons
explanation and a causal explanation, for a reasons
explanation is not wholly adequate if we can only
claim that I <u>have</u> a reason. We want to be able to
say not only that I have a reason but that I believe
so-and-so because of my reason, and we are able to
claim this only if we integrate a causal account and
a reasons account. I may take my reason to justify
my belief, and the cause to explain my having it,
but my justification will ring hollow if what causes
my belief has nothing to do with my reasons, that is
to say, if exploring my reasons would not lead me to
the cause. I think that this will be readily
apparent, if it is not already, when we examine
rationalizations, which are reasons which do compete
with causes.

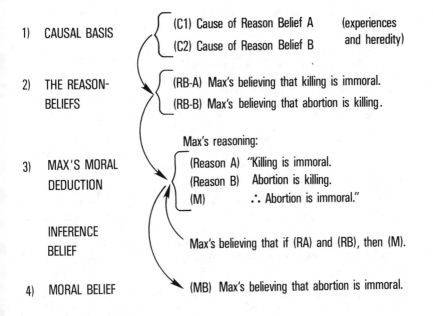

Figure 1.
An arrow indicates that one item is a causal
condition of another.

The schema illustrates the relations between the causes of and reasons for Max's moral belief when he believes what he believes because of his reasons, that is to say, in a case in which a causal explanation and a reasons explanation complement one another. The solution relies on my claim that if C causes a person to believe the premises of a valid deductive argument, C usually also causes him to believe the conclusion. Now it is clear that if C causes me to believe that abortion is killing and that killing is immoral, we cannot deduce from this that I believe abortion is immoral. Even if we add the premise that I believe the argument is valid, we still cannot deduce that I believe the conclusion. Nevertheless, it is in general true that if C causes a person to believe "killing is immoral" and "abortion is killing," and he believes that those premises entail "abortion is immoral," then C causes him to believe that abortion is immoral. Since this is an empirical and not a logical "if...then" we should not be surprised if we find exceptions to it.

In Figure 1, Max's moral deduction (3) is causally dependent on his reason-beliefs (2) (and hence on _their_ causes) only in the sense that unless he was caused to believe the premises of the deduction he could not, in virtue of the deduction, believe the conclusion. Of course, a deduction _qua_ propositional entity is not caused and its validity is not caused. What is caused by Cl and C2 is his taking the deduction to have acceptable premises. Max's reason, i.e., the deductive argument in (3), is not merely ornamental in this chain of causes: If the deduction is invalid he will not make the move from his reason beliefs (2) to his moral belief (4) unless he believes it is valid. In most cases, Cl and C2 will cause Max to believe abortion is immoral only if he believes the argument in (3) is valid and he will believe the argument in (3) is valid only if it _is_ valid.

The schema asserts that (a) there exists a cause of Max's moral belief, (b) Max has a reason that entails his moral belief, (c) both the reason and the cause are necessary for his having it, and (d) the reason is in harmony with the cause not just in the sense that they are compatible but also in the sense that tracing back his reasons leads us to the cause. Given all of this we can say that the cause of his reason-beliefs is the same as the cause of his moral belief and that the reason he gives is "the real reason" why he believes what he believes.

   6.2   Rationalizing.   What should we say when someone believes M but not because of his reason? It is an issue that concerns the rationality of believers, as distinct from the rationality of what is believed, and it is important to an overall understanding of moral reasoning. Consider the notion of "rationalization," which the 1966 RANDOM HOUSE DICTIONARY defines as "to invent plausible explanations for acts, opinions, etc., that are actually based on other causes." Since initial intuitions about its meaning as well as the dictionary suggest a contrast between reasons and causes, rationalization is a good concept in terms of which to continue our inquiry.

   Let us briefly reconsider actions. Suppose Max has been given an ultimatum to finish his doctoral dissertation this year. He has a history of procrastinating, working only sporadically during the past months, and now he sits in Larry's Bar each night drinking beer. He says, "I've been working hard and now I go to the bar because I need a rest." We might feel justified in claiming that is not the real reason why he goes to the bar each night: He is rationalizing; the real reason is that he doesn't want to work on his dissertation. We need to distinguish a reason he might give from his reason, that is, from the reason he accepts. He might give any reason, e.g., "I've decided to become an alcoholic," if his purpose is to be flippant to a bore, or whatever. This is not the real reason why he goes to the bar. Neither is the real reason the reason he actually accepts. The reason he accepts is what he thinks is the real reason why he goes to the bar, but when we claim he is rationalizing we claim he is incorrect, that something else is the real reason why he goes, something which is neither the reason he gives nor the reason he accepts.

   I am inclined to think that, in general, our intellectual self-respect requires us to believe

155

that the reasons we accept as explanatory or justifying are what made us perform the action or hold the belief for which they are reasons. This appears to be so for all reason-giving whether it be reasons in support of nonmoral beliefs, reasons for action, or moral reasons. We very much want to think that what makes us act or believe something is closely tied to our reasons. If I think a certain fact makes me believe the house next door is vacant, for example the fact that it is boarded up, I almost invariably also believe that fact justifies my belief; and, in turn, that its being boarded up makes me believe it is boarded up; and ultimately, that it is boarded up because it is vacant. If not, if for example, I came to believe that a hypnotic suggestion made me believe the house is vacant, then I must admit that my belief is (or was) irrational in the sense that what made me hold it is irrelevant to what could warrant or justify it.

In the case of action it is plain that Max's own reason why he goes to the bar is what he thinks brings him there, makes him go. He intends us to understand this when he honestly tells us why he goes. If we are correct about why he goes, he is mistaken. In the case of moral belief, if Harry believes premarital sex is immoral for such and such reasons, he thinks and hopes it is because of his reasons that he believes it, and he would be loathe to admit otherwise. Nevertheless, we know we can be mistaken: We know that when someone accepts a reason why the house is vacant, or why he went to the bar, or why premarital sex is immoral, that in each case something else unrelated to his reason may be what made him believe or act as he did: His reason may have no place in the causal chain that culminates in his action or belief. When a person is mistaken in this way I shall call the reason a rationalization. After all, to say one does (or believes) X because one wants (or believes) Y is to make an empirical claim which like any other can be false.

Some moral beliefs are a person's ultimate ones, beliefs he does not support with reasons at all. These will have "mere causes," that is to say, causes not themselves reason beliefs. It might be thought that because ultimately we arrive at "mere causes" morality must be irrational. Perhaps non-rational in a certain sense. But it would be wrong to call beliefs irrational when the "mere causes" are deep causes, the beliefs they cause are not crazy and are related to our nature and evolutionary history, and they do not depend on errors of reasoning or fact. This view may displease philosophers more than any other professional group, perhaps because sheer reasoning rather than the accumulation of facts is their profession. Philosophers would like to prove that reason alone can supply motives and goals because they see themselves as stewards of the power of reasoning: It is their sword, arguments are their battles, and whatever limits the role of reasoning in the world limits them.

In the schema of Section 6.1 a person held a moral belief because of his reasons. How do reasons relate to causes when he does not believe M because of his reasons, when his reasons are rationalizations and something else is the cause--his fears, desires, or certain experiences? When we give reasons we implicitly claim that we (and not just our beliefs) are rational, and lay claim to a certain kind of self-knowledge about the genesis of our moral beliefs. When we rationalize, these implicit claims are false. Consider President Nixon's claim, during the months before he resigned, that on grounds of executive privilege and the constitutional separation of powers it would be wrong to surrender his clandestine White House tape recordings. In terms of our theory there are at least four alternative hypotheses about the reasons for and causes of Nixon's belief: insincerity, non-rationalization, rationalization, and overdetermination.

(1) Nixon was insincere: He did not really believe he morally ought to withhold the Watergate tapes; he simply did not want to yield them. This is hypocrisy, which is not rationalization but shades off into it; the closer we think his deception is to self-deception the more we are inclined to call this a case of rationalization. But qua hypocrisy there isn't any issue about the cause of a moral belief because there isn't any moral belief.

157

(2) He neither lied nor rationalized: His belief that he should keep the tapes is not dependent on his fear of impeachment or prosecution. He thought executive privilege overrode the prosecutor's claim that he needed the tapes to prepare criminal prosecutions, and overrode the Congress' claim that they needed the tapes for an impeachment investigation, and he would have thought this even if his own position and reputation were not at stake. Given this, we can hypothesize that what did make him believe he should keep the tapes is to be found by tracing back his reasons, through fidelity to the constitutional requirement of separation of powers, etc., to whatever it is that caused him, and presumably many other people too, to subscribe to those basic ethical principles with which he would defend the constitution. Therefore he believed he should keep the tapes because of the reasons he gave. The chain of causes is in fact just what Nixon would think it is: It is the chain of reason beliefs that corresponds to his chain of reasons.

(3) Nixon was rationalizing: His belief that he ought to withhold the tapes is caused by his fear of impeachment and disgrace. I assume that his principles about the importance of executive privilege and the separation of powers are independent of his fears and that he held these principles all along. But without his fears he would not have thought that keeping the tapes was required by these principles. What he thinks makes him believe he should keep the tapes is one thing, what actually does make him believe it is another thing.

His desire to avoid impeachment is what makes him classify withholding the tapes as a legitimate case of honoring the requirement of separation of powers. Paraphrasing Charles Stevenson,[2] we might call this a persuasive classification; when Nixon is rationalizing he does not know that what makes him accept this classification and what makes him accept the moral belief the classification is employed to support are the same thing, namely his fears. Persuasive classification plays on the vagueness, indeterminacy, or at least, controversiality of calling X a case of Y, for example, calling a two day old human embryo a person. It is more reasonable to call such classifications arbitrary, stipulative, or unclear rather than simply erroneous.

Rationalizers commonly make problematic or unreasonable judgments of degree, quantity, likelihood, or sufficiency: "It would be too expensive," "There is too great a chance it will break," "Someone could trip on it and sue you," and so on. Such judgments seldom can be empirically refuted, for the claim is not just that the probability of X (e.g., that the suspect had a gun) is Y, but that probability Y is enough or suffices for there being, e.g., a case of imminent danger.

It may be tempting to think that a criterion of rationalization is that one first acquires a moral belief and only later produces reasons for it. This would be a mistake. A person may hold a moral belief out of gut reaction, vague intuition, for no reason at all, or he may defend it with rationalizations, and only later discover reasons that are not rationalizations. Cases of this sort are common: A child is trained to have certain moral beliefs and later discovers satisfactory reasons for some of them. In this situation two distinct causes may have been necessary for him now to have the moral belief. I want to say he is not rationalizing if the reason beliefs he acquires now are necessary for his moral belief and the cause that lay in his early training is no longer necessary. We can call these causal replacement cases.

For instance, suppose that Charles Colson, having just found Christ, ran to Nixon and said "Fear not!," and Nixon feared not. This provides the crucial test, for even if we suppose that his fears are what originally produced his moral belief (and his moral reasonsing), if his belief can survive the loss of his fears we have good grounds for thinking he now holds the belief because of his reasons and is not rationalizing. Rationalization depends on whether or not the present causal situation is what one thinks or implies it is; it does not depend on what the original cause of belief is or when one acquired reasons.

(4) Overdetermination: If Nixon's moral belief is overdetermined he believes he should keep the

tapes because of his reasons and also because of his
fears; and moreover, we do not suppose that his
fears produce his reasons. In overdetermination
his reason beliefs and his fears are independent
causes in the sense that they are not members of the
same causal chain. If his fears had caused his
reason beliefs which in turn caused his moral
belief, we would not have overdetermination because
in a case of overdetermination each cause, without
the other, suffices to produce the belief. Overdetermination perhaps should not be called rationalization, for he believes M because of his reason.
Nevertheless, if we know that Nixon's moral belief
was overdetermined we can say of him, "He would have
believed M anyway, even if he did not have reasons."
Ideally, people not only want it to be true that
they believe things because of their reasons, they
also want it to be false that they would believe
those things in the absence of their reasons.

Rationalizers mistakenly think they believe
so-and-so because of their reasons; with regard to
this part of their moral repertoires they lack a
certain kind of self-knowledge. Someone's belief is
irrational if he doesn't know why he holds it and,
if he acts on it, is ignorant of why he acts as he
does. It is not that our moral beliefs are irrational if we do not know their ultimate, non-intentional
causes; rather, we want the principles to which we
appeal to be relevant links in what produces our
beliefs. The ultimate origins of our passions and
values are partly mysteries, hidden in millions of
years of prehuman and early human evolution. As I
shall argue, this ensures at least some measure of
cross-cultural agreement. That Man has a nature
that determines our deepest wants and aversions, and
therefore our deepest values, is not a threat to our
rationality; but whether our values depend on what
we think they do certainly is relevant to our
rationality. It is possible we never can be
completely certain we are not rationalizing. The
situation is not unlike that in which Kant admits a
person cannot be completely certain he acts for the
sake of duty and hence from an unselfish motive,
rather than merely in accord with duty.

If I abandon my rationalizations without replac-
ing them with anything I am left with a belief that

I think results from a mere cause. Such a belief
would be a monstrosity, something that ought not to
be my belief at all, because a cause, qua cause,
does not warrant belief. The idea of a cause is
just the idea of efficacy, of the power to bring
something about. If a cause produces belief, which
is the idea that something is warranted, true or
justified, it apparently can do so in the absence of
any warrant, reason, or justification at all. It
comforts us to think the reason for a belief is
identical with its cause precisely because it implies that when we abandon our reason, its effect,
the belief, will disappear: If one's reason is the
cause, a belief that loses its reason loses its
cause. Thinking of reasons as causes therefore
protects our image of rationality but it makes
irrational belief more difficult to explain, or
better, it treats all irrationality as justificatory
error, as cases of having faulty reasons which,
faulty though they are, still are what make us hold
our beliefs. What causes our beliefs sometimes
includes nothing we would think warrants them, but--
and this is the grain of truth in rationalistic
moral psychology--rationalization shows that something in us makes us go to great lengths not to
admit it.

Why, when I discover I lack a reason, do I tend
to abandon my belief? If what causes me to believe
capital punishment is justified is (among other
things) my belief that it is a better deterrent, the
answer is obvious: When the cause of my belief
operates through my reason beliefs, then when I
abandon the reason I abandon the belief. A person
none of whose moral beliefs are rationalizations in
my sense will of necessity reject them when he
rejects his reasons for them (with the exception of
those that are overdetermined).

This is the easy part of the answer to the
question of why knowledge liberates; it is the only
part of the answer that the rationalist moral
psychologist can provide: We can understand how
rejecting a reason is followed by rejecting the
belief when it implies rejecting the belief's
cause. But why should exposing a rationalization
effect my belief when it was ornamental, causally
irrelevant, in the first place? The problem is like

that raised by psychiatry patients. I would guess that most educated patients at one time or another ask their doctors how learning why they do X should help them to stop doing X. Given that it is true that C causes X, why should merely coming to know that C causes X make C cease to cause X? So too, if C (Nixon's fears, or such and such early experience) actually is the cause of belief M, giving up one's rationalization is just recognizing as not a cause what never was a cause. If beliefs can have brute causes, not only is Platonic rational determinism false, but it also seems that reasons have no edge, qua belief producers, over mindless, brute causes.

If giving up the rationalization does make one give up M, it appears as though the rationalization was necessary for it after all, which would defeat what I have said about rationalization as well as the view expressed in the dictionary. A rationalization, by definition, is not a "real reason" why one believes something; why, then, does it behave like one? We seem faced with the dilemma of either admitting that the rationalizer's reasons are causes when we have better evidence that they are not and that some fear is the cause, or admitting that unmasking a rationalization cannot affect belief even though we have good evidence that it does.

Difficult as it may be to understand how knowledge liberates, there appear to be clear cases in which it does. Suppose that the hypnotist says to me, "When I snap my fingers you will wake up and believe your boss is trying to poison you." He snaps his fingers, I awake, believe my boss is trying to poison me, and produce rationalizations such as, "He thinks I want his job" and "Why else is he inviting me to dinner after all these years?" Now suppose I am told about the hypnosis and I tell you, "While I was hypnotized the hypnotist said to me, 'When I snap my fingers you will wake up and believe...(etc.)'; now I know why I believe my boss is trying to poison me, and I won't let him succeed." Does not this response go beyond the merely stupid and approach the psychologically impossible? What almost invariably really happens is that when I abandon the rationalizations and discover that my belief had a "mere cause," I abandon the belief.

162

A partial explanation is that the "mere cause" that produces my belief is also what produces my rationalizations: My belief and my rationalizations stand or fall together, they have a common cause. So knowledge that I was rationalizing is not what liberates, but rather, I abandon my rationalizations because I already have abandoned, or am in the process of abandoning, the belief they supported. But the main problem about the apparent efficacy of reason remains and I do not know the solution: Why should discovering that a belief is unwarranted have any tendency to remove or loosen a cause, given that the cause is there in the first place?

6.3 <u>Nature, Nurture, and the Normative.</u> I have talked enough about meaning, arguments, and reasons--about what, so to speak, happens up front in ethics--and I have discussed the general nature of the relation between reasons and causes. Now the hints and suggestions about causal matters need to be brought together. I would like to be able to build a bridge between our reasoned moral life and our biological nature. The deeper and more interesting causal hypotheses are genetic ones, both because they suggest that one is getting to the bottom of things and because they offer the possibility of discovering "moral universals" in the sense of predispositions to have values that are cross-cultural and perhaps common to the species. The only creditable way to proceed is to trace a plausible causal chain from a hypothesized gene to some present person's actual moral belief. This I shall attempt to do, although the detailed examination of human nature and the form it imparts to our norms and social life must be left to another occasion.

First, however, something needs to be said about the often confused distinction between nature and nurture, between what is biologically innate and what is acquired. "Nature/nurture" is one of those stark and simple dualisms that begs to be slain by those of us who believe nature is too subtle to tolerate simple dichotomies. What I think is the sensible position--and it is also the view of many contemporary evolutionary biologists--is that neither one's genes nor one's environment by themselves are capable of causing anything, but that jointly they cause everything we are and do. This claim should displease only those who believe that moral agents are unmoved movers, since genes and environment, by stipulation, divide up all of the ordinary candidates for causes that there are. By itself, a gene is a dispositional cause: in a certain range of environments a certain effect will occur and if the gene is absent the effect will not occur unless some other cause plays the same role. A gene is a cause of this effect--a bodily structure or bit of behavior; and if it is a cause that especially interests us, we may call it the cause.

Genes and environments are causally symmetrical: Each is a dispositional cause, impotent without the contribution of the other. Given a particular environment as background there are possible genetic combinations under which a certain behavior will occur, such as collecting postage stamps or a particular performance on an IQ test. Conversely, given a particular genetic makeup as background there is a possible environment in which someone will collect postage stamps. Vary either the genes or the environment in the right way and he will not. We can say the same thing of any behavior however instinctual or noninstinctual it is commonly thought to be; genes and environment always are individually necessary conditions and, if biological determinism is true, jointly sufficient conditions. In the postage stamp case the genetic causes, so far as we know and excepting genetic disease and retardation, are so invariant relative to the environmental causes that there are no occasions when it is of interest to mention them. That is the only reason why we call stamp collecting acquired rather than instinctive. When we call just one of these causal components the cause and thus claim that a behavior is innate or acquired, we are spotlighting a cause that interests us because it is dramatically variable, or dramatically invariable, or manipulable, and we are reserving the notion of causal precondition or background for what, in terms of our interest, lies in the shadow.

Neither evolution nor natural selection need be genetic or even biological notions. Stars, artistic styles, human cultures, and the internal combustion

164

engine have, in various senses of the word, evolved. For this reason it is important to distinguish the biological notion from the more general "Spencerian" notion of evolution. The biological concept is genetic, the Spencerian need not be and it includes both cultural evolution and biological evolution as subspecies. One important difference is that in nonbiological evolution acquired characteristics can be transmitted to a new instance or individual and in biological evolution they cannot.

However, culture does not make our form of life "less biological" than that of other creatures; culture is merely a special kind of environment--one that progressively changes. Suppose that in environment $\underline{A}$ orb spiders spin webs of 72 turns and in environment $\underline{B}$ a human society has a feudal political system. If for the next generation the environments change to $\underline{A}'$ and $\underline{B}'$, the spiders may spin 50-turn webs and the humans move toward capitalism. The new spider behavior is no less instinctive than the old, in spite of its environmental cause, for the old behavior was no less environmentally determined than the new. The same is true for the humans. If the total environments reverted to $\underline{A}$ and $\underline{B}$, spider behavior and human behavior would revert to what they were before. But the point is that the humans' environment includes a culture and we find it very difficult to imagine that part of our environment reverting to what it was before. To say that humans have a culture means that our history continually effects us and makes a complete reversion to a past condition causally improbable, however cyclical the climate and other aspects of nature might be. This is a very important difference between people and spiders: Spiders have to start from scratch every generation. For humans there is a new environment each generation that is caused by the past generations, and we call this cultural evolution. In the absence of new patterns of differential reproduction or new mutagens in our packaged food this cultural evolution will not produce genetic change. Nevertheless it is just as "hereditary" and simultaneously just as "acquired" as would be progressive changes in web spinning brought about by progressive changes in spider environments.

What should we say about the evolution of altruism, of English, or of our sense of retributive or distributive justice? Political thinkers and social scientists are wary of biologists' promises to provide genetical explanations of human attitudes and values. The nub of the issue is not causal determinism--social scientists hardly can be said to eschew that--but the fact that genetic causes, unlike cultural ones, are beyond the reach of social engineers and moral revolutionaries. Social reformers hope to tinker with society and thus change people's values, but they cannot (now) change our values by tinkering with our genes. Hence they understandably perceive sociobiological hypotheses as threats, as competition. In addition, social and political reformers fear the old arguments: Man is by nature warlike, competitive, acquisitive, or male dominant, and "therefore" these traits cannot be changed (or should not be changed). But now these ancient sophistries would be dressed up in the impressive mathematics of population genetics and we would be told that not only our behavior but our very judgments about that behavior are "from Nature."

The sophistry lies not in the genetical hypotheses about our nature but in the inference that we cannot (or even should not) do anything about it. The malleability of human beliefs and behavior is no greater or less than what we have for centuries observed it to be. A celibate priest should not find his celibacy more irksome upon being told, for the first time, that his sexual urges have a genetic basis. So too, it should not frustrate a socialist to be told that Man is genetically disposed to be warlike, acquisitive and competitive (if indeed there is any truth to this); he may think socialism necessary because he believes that already. If it were true we are genetically disposed to be aggressive and male dominant, this might be a useful truth about ourselves: those of us who do not favor those traits (but perhaps at times feel their pull) would now have better reasons for intensively educating children to the harm of aggression and male dominance. It is not news that civilization does battle, often successfully, with aspects of "our nature." Moreover, the claim that a biological (and not just cultural) evolution of moral attitudes implies the inevitability (or even the justification) of the social or political status quo is silly. One wants to ask, which status quo and when? That in China or Cuba, or in America, England, or the Rome of Emperor Heliogabalus? One need not reject hypotheses about the evolution of attitudes and values in order to reject claims of inevitability, one need only read the newspaper and study a little history.

A relatively clear but limited way of reintroducing the notions of "innate" and "acquired" is the following. When we ask if a pattern of behavior or kind of moral belief is innate we are not asking if its causes include evolved genetic ones. The causes always include evolved genetic ones. Nor are we asking if it cannot be changed; it always can if we want to badly enough. We instead ask either of two different questions: (a) Are people with this moral belief genetically different from otherwise similar people without it? Or (b) are the genetic causes of sufficient penetrance that the moral belief, or ones very similar to it, is shared by nearly all of Mankind? These questions are genuine and important ones.

Suppose we answer the first question affirmatively: People with a certain kind of moral attitude tend to be genetically different from other people. There are several reasons for doubting this. First, it is probable that Man is now sufficiently master of his environment that an enormous diversity of behavior will not be biologically selected against. This mastery includes the ability to produce surplus food and eliminate big predatory cats. Human cultures can "afford" practices that otherwise would make them biologically unfit. For example, the support of large numbers of invalids, aged, and indigent probably would be biologically maladaptive in ancient, primitive societies. The 19th century social Darwinians thought helping the poor was maladaptive in modern American society and that the practice would doom us; but even practices that are economically inefficient and make us all a little poorer do not necessarily make us have fewer or more sickly children.

Moreover, is behavior that is disliked or disapproved in a culture, such as sloth or criminal behavior, biologically selected against? We are easily

167

tempted to think that industriousness (in our culture) is selected for and thievery selected against
because we approve the former and try to diminish
the latter. But do industrious people have more
children than other people, or thieves fewer
children, as they must if there is to be biological
selection? This would have to be determined case by
case and the answers are not obvious in advance.

Finally, even if a kind of behavior or kind of
culture is selected against, as measured by fewer
offspring or curtailed survival, need the process be
biological? For all we know, cultures can surmount
or succumb to competition from other cultures
without altering the overall genetic makeup of the
survivors, and this simply because the competing
cultures were not genetically different in the first
place. Carthage might have destroyed Rome without
our having to suppose that Scipio's, Hannibal's, or
anybody's, genes were different from what they
were. People with a certain socially disapproved
behavioral trait may have fewer children than
others, and in that case we could speak of selection
in the biological sense, if, in addition, we had
independent evidence that those people were genetically different from people without the trait.

Prehistoric Man and his hominid ancestors lived
during a time of "hard selection," that is, under
strong selective pressures such that minute advantages would have genetic consequences for future
generations. As I have suggested, modern Man, like
the Gypsy moth, lives in a period (perhaps tem-
porary) of soft selection, and therefore can afford
behavior his ancestors could not afford. If selection was hard back then and is soft now, what
emerges is the hypothesis that genes which causally
contribute to important, species wide moral beliefs
were fixed very long ago.

The genetic causes of behavior, while varying as
we would expect among individuals, are thought by
many to be similar for all fairly large groups of
people. If so, behavioral and normative diversity
between groups is due to environment, which seems to
deprive the biologist of a role in explaining cultural diversity. Yet, suppose that social scientists
have had a hard time explaining behaviors A, B, and

C, as found in three different cultures. The socio-biologists' hypotheses might help explain A, B, and C by finding in them something common and adaptive, or alternatively, by postulating a common human need or function which, combining with three different environments, intelligibly yields three modes of behavior which share no significant common features.

The second sense in which we can sensibly ask if a normative trait is "by nature" is more exciting because it is more likely to be true: Are there genetic causes that explain moral sentiments shared by nearly all of Mankind? Hypotheses of this second kind imply a relative permanence and near univer-sality for certain moral sentiments such as altruism and incest taboo but not for others. These hypotheses would, if true, refute the view that morality is arbitrary and that people can adopt whatever moral beliefs they please. Yet the fears of social reformers focus on this very point, for such knowledge might tell us that some kinds of moral attitudes are going to be more difficult to extirpate, or to cultivate, than others. Must a moral messiah be told to choose his doctrines in the light of evolutionary history if he wishes to be successful? Perhaps so, if the moral re-education he has in mind is sufficiently drastic. But, we do not need biologists to tell us what this is; we already know from history and observation what we are likely to be able to change in people.

6.4 How Genes Can Cause Moral Beliefs. Are there hereditary moral universals, an "instinctive human morality"? I think there is, but even its very possibility is in need of explanation. To begin, how does one forge a chain of causes that begins with evolutionary considerations and ends with a moral judgment? The important but complex cases concern innate human sociality and the mix of collectivist and individualist values we evolved to be disposed to feel. But that is a long story, and another project, so I shall attempt to explain a simpler chain of causes in which the last link is someone's saying sincerely, "incest is immoral."

Cultural anthropologists are generally agreed that what they call incest taboo is common to all human cultures. It takes different forms in different cultures, including variations in strictness as well as in what gets counted as incest. Thus not all cultures agree about marriage between first cousins. I shall assume this diversity is due to different environmental causes. We should remember that incest taboo is the joint product of genes and environment and that to say it has a genetic cause is to spotlight a cause that interests us. Now a taboo need not be a moral belief. Certain social taboos are not matters of morality, but on my theory some of them are. The only admission I require for the moment is that the belief common in our society, that incest between close relatives is wrong, is the kind of thing we call a taboo in "primitive" societies: we and they are both opposed to incest although it is called immorality in our culture and called (by our anthropologists) a mere taboo in theirs.

Every human being is thought to carry between three and eight lethal recessive genes and it is plausible to suppose that lethal recessives are carried by nearly all sexually reproducing animals. An animal that receives a double dose of one of these genes, that is to say, receives it from both parents, is likely to die before it has offspring. If an animal carries a lethal gene and it mates with a close relative, the statistical likelihood that its mate also carries the gene is a function of the coefficient of relation between them: For any non-sex-linked gene you carry, the likelihood that your parent or sibling has it too is 1/2, that your half sib has it is 1/4, and that your cousin has it is 1/8. And if both parents do have the bad recessive gene, the odds that any given child will receive it from both of them is 1/4. The risk that incestuous mating will produce offspring with genetic disease is very high compared with the risk associated with mating between non-relatives. Consequently if we postulate two similar animal populations in similar environments, with the exception that in the one incest is practiced considerably more frequently than in the other, the incestuous one will be less fit than the nonincestuous one; the incestuous one will be selected against in evolution and if the two populations compete for resources we can expect the non-incestuous one to replace the incestuous one. As we should expect from nature, there are exceptions, for example, some insects whose unusual ecological niches make incestuous reproductive strategies the best ones.

We should expect to find behavioral mechanisms in surviving animal populations that sharply reduce the likelihood of incestuous matings taking place. And we do. This is simply a matter of natural selection; we needn't suppose that an animal understands genetics or knows that sex has something to do with reproduction. I want to describe a few of these incest avoidance mechanisms. The first is abandonment. A moth lays its eggs and flies away, a sea turtle buries its eggs on the beach and swims away. The moths that emerge from the pupae and the turtles that hatch from the eggs then disperse, and the likelihood that one of these animals will mate with a parent or sibling is slight. If a moth or turtle population did things differently such that the odds in favor of incest were higher, that population would be at a selective disadvantage, other things being equal, relative to the populations we observe. Abandonment obviously will not do if the young require parental care, as is the case with birds and mammals. Consequently we should expect alternate mechanisms that accomplish the same end. What we find is that sometimes the young are ejected from the nest before they reach sexual maturity, sometimes they tend to leave on their own, and sometimes the parent or parents leave when the young are able to fend for themselves but prior to sexual maturity.

A few animals, however, tend to remain together in family groups well past the sexual maturity of the young, humans being one example and the chimpanzee another, as reported in Jane van Lawick-Goodall's studies of chimpanzees in Tanzania.[3] Since the argument for the relative fitness of non-incestuous populations applies to humans and chimpanzees we should expect yet another incest avoidance mechanism to have evolved. But it is not immediately obvious what it would be since nothing so gross as abandonment or ejection is to be generally observed. Jane Goodall describes a female chimp called Flo who walked around accompanied by her sexually mature son. When she was in estrus Flo was spectacularly promiscuous and mated with all the mature males around her, with the exception of her son. A plausible hypothesis is an incest avoidance mechanism that works through the emotions and requires a level of intelligence not found in moths or turtles. What I suggest is an aversive reaction toward incest with parents or siblings--a disposition to have either negative feelings or a lack of interest.

We should be clear what this requires. A chimpanzee need not know what a sibling or parent is in the biological sense, but it must be able to respond to the social roles parents and siblings usually play and it probably must be able to reidentify individuals. Thus a chimpanzee is able to pick out individuals who as a matter of fact are likely to be sibs or parents without having the capacity to know them as sibs or parents. This is important because the aversive reaction in humans regarding incest can be assumed to have evolved during our pre-human ancestry when individuals lacked the concepts of sib, parent, and incest. Some corroboration of the hypothesis that human incest aversion is triggered by the social roles close kin usually have rather than by actual knowledge of kinship relations is provided by studies of children brought up in Israeli Kibbutzim.[4] Unrelated Kibbutz children lived together like brothers and sisters. They never married each other. It is not that they called it incest, for they knew it would not be; they said things such as "He (or she) is like a brother (or sister) to me."

A common misconception is that genetic causes are invariant causes. Social workers deal with incest and attempted incest all the time. But then neither do the incest avoidance mechanisms of moths and turtles work flawlessly. Genetic causes can be absent or diminished in particular individuals, and when they are present will be defeated, modified, or enhanced depending on the environment. We should think of a genetic cause as a "prima facie" cause: it is really there, but the actual outcome depends on all the causes that are at work.

The argument so far has been a sociobiological one. Now the theory of moral belief I outlined permits the next step in the process of tracing a causal chain from selective forces in evolution to present day moral beliefs. The theory says moral beliefs are aversive or supportive dispositions that bear the marks of the moral. The incest avoidance mechanism hypothesized for humans, unlike sea turtles, is an aversive disposition toward matings that as a matter of fact are likely to be incestuous. In order for this disposition to be a moral belief it must have the descriptive features I call the marks of the moral and it must be conceptualized, that is, expressible in language under some such term as "incest," all of which implies that it must be taken up and reinforced by a culture. I think these conditions are met. Incest opposition has a general appeal in moral communities, it concerns human behavior, and "ought" judgments concerning incest are universalizable and override considerations of self-interest and manners.

It is of no great importance to the theory (although it does matter to my own worldview) whether the social scientists or the sociobiologists are right about incest taboo or altruism. The important point is that moral beliefs, when they are understood as special kinds of aversive or supportive dispositions, are the kinds of things that can result from the causes social scientists as well as evolutionary biologists postulate. The cultural anthropologists might have the better answer--viz., that incest is universally condemned because out-marriage has social and economic advantages--although I doubt it. The social scientists' explanations in general have less explanatory power because they do not go so far back in time and do not as readily connect up with the behavior of other animals.

More important for ethics are evolutionary explanations of altruism. Behavior that increases Darwinian fitness need not be what commonly is called selfish, for animals that sacrifice themselves for their offspring may have relatively great Darwinian fitness. Neither is self-interested behavior always compatible with fitness, for example if an animal eats its prospective mates or its newborn young; doing so may prolong its own survival but by definition it lacks fitness because its genes will not be passed on to a new generation. Whether or not we think classical Darwinism can explain how altruistic behavior can evolve by natural selection partly depends on whether we count sacrifice for our children as selfish or altruistic. At most, it is a limited kind of altruism. It would not provide an evolutionary, genetic, basis for altruism toward strangers and hence would not go very far toward providing an evolutionary account of the origin of morality.

An often used example shows the difficulty of accounting for a broader altruism by means of classical Darwinian theory. Birds of some flocking species give alarm cries when they see an approaching predator. This enables the flock to flee sooner than it might otherwise, but it also increases the likelihood the predator will notice and catch the bird who gave the alarm cry. Some of these birds do have counter-measures--cries that are acoustically obscure or even ventriloquistic and thus hard to locate spatially--but it is not thought that in general the defense negates the risk. Flocks whose members regularly give alarm signals will have greater fitness than otherwise similar flocks. But how could this behavior ever begin to become widespread in a flock? If a low mutation rate or particular gene combinations cause a small number of birds to give alarm cries, they will be more likely than their silent comrades to be eaten before they can reproduce; the trait will be selected against and their genes will not proliferate through the flock. An analogous objection to the fitness of human altruism is obvious, for all altruism implies taking risks, however small the risk might be.

The bird example is one way to illustrate the problem of group selection: a group that gives warning cries will be fitter than a group that does not, but individuals in the group who give warning cries will be less fit than individuals who do not. How, then, can the warning cry genes come to predominate in the group? We could think of the warning cries as social morality and the silent birds, if proportionately few, as free riders, parasites on the system and thereby best off. The squawkers, if proportionately few, would be martyrs and would not, it seems, become more numerous.

W. D. Hamilton's 1964 theory of kin selection is a celebrated and widely accepted attempt to solve this problem.[5] Hamilton's theory is built around his notion of inclusive fitness. Consider the birds again and a rather artificial example. A bird, Harry, gives a warning cry with the result that he is eaten by the hawk but two of his siblings escape who otherwise would not have escaped. As we saw earlier, each sib has, on the average, 1/2 of Harry's genes. Since the likelihood that each sib carries the warning cry genes is 1/2, and Harry saves two sibs by sacrificing himself, he has done as well in passing on that trait as he would had he sacrificed two sibs to save himself. Harry's behavior plainly reduces his own fitness but it does not reduce inclusive fitness, which is the sum of his own fitness and the product of his effect on the fitness of his relatives and the various coefficients of relation.

In small populations containing high proportions of relatives it is easy to see how self-sacrificial behavior can be selected for: while an altruistic act reduces the altruist's fitness it can increase inclusive fitness by benefitting a sufficient number of relatives. The principle is the same when a mother takes risks for the children who bear her genes, but it is a puzzle why most earlier Darwinians did not think of applying it to relatives other than children, exceptions to this being J.B.S. Haldane, and Darwin who hints at it. Hamilton summarizes his view as follows:

> ...for a hereditary tendency to perform an action of this kind to evolve the benefit to a sib must average at least twice the loss to the individual, the benefit to a half-sib must be at least four times the loss, to a cousin eight times and so on. To express the matter more vividly, in the world of our model organisms, whose behavior is determined strictly by genotype, we expect to find that no one is prepared to sacrifice his life for any single person but that everyone will sacrifice it when he

175

can thereby save more than two brothers, or four half-brothers, or eight first cousins....[6]

A second influencial argument for the genetical evolution of altruistic behavior and attitudes comes from Robert Trivers. The idea behind Trivers' theory of reciprocal altruism is that altruistic behavior can enhance individual fitness if it tends to lead to its reciprocation.[7] Trivers argues that if an altruist is genetically disposed to help only other altruists he will have greater fitness than either an egoist or an altruist who is willing to help anyone. Suppose a drowning person has a 1/2 chance of dying if not assisted, less than a 1/20 chance of dying if assisted, and the rescuer has a 1/20 chance of dying. If considerations of kin selection are laid aside this sort of altruistic risk taking will be selected against. But if the rescued person is an altruist too and, in addition, is more inclined to rescue altruists (including the rescuer when he needs it), the rescuer is increasing his own fitness by his altruistic act.

Hence Trivers implies that the small but certain risk required by the altruistic act is outweighed by the great though uncertain gain of future assistance. In general, the cost to an altruist is less than the benefit to the recipient--altruism typically producing a net benefit to the altruist/recipient couple. This contrasts interestingly with criminal/victim transactions in which, usually, the gain to the criminal is less than the loss to the victim, producing a net loss to the criminal/victim couple. This shows that virtue is better than vice.

The selective superiority of reciprocal altruism over both promiscuous altruism and total selfishness presupposes that the animals involved are intelligent enough to remember who helped them and who didn't. However, this requirement would seem to apply only to altruists who disappear from the scene to reappear elsewhere, as hominids would, and thus need to be recognized; for Trivers also applies the model to cleaner fish whose large predatory partners are not intelligent. Reciprocal altruism also seems to require that the group be small enough for individuals to meet each other again fairly often.

What is needed in addition is an explanation of how genes for reciprocal altruism could survive early in their history when there were very few reciprocal altruists and the likelihood of two of them meeting more than once was slight. One possible way such an explanation might go is the following. We begin with Hamilton's notion of kin selection: let us suppose there has evolved altruistic behavior which increases inclusive fitness at a cost to individual fitness. There must have evolved mechanisms to prevent animals that lack the ability to recognize kin from sacrificing themselves too often for non-relatives. For example, reserving one's altruism for those within a certain spatial or social perimeter might do this. It is the same mechanism that is used for incest avoidance. Once this kind of restrictive altruism became established, those who helped someone would often be kin, and thus it would work to the advantage of the altruistic genes to help helpers, for the very same kinds of reasons that it would work to the advantage of the altruistic genes to help those who were close spatially or socially. In other words one could become disposed, purely on grounds of enhanced inclusive fitness, to treat as brothers all people who act like brothers.

Now suppose I encounter a non-relative; if we are each disposed to help the other merely because he is nearby, and I help him, my act contributes neither to inclusive fitness (because he is not a relative) nor to my individual fitness (because his behavior is unaffected by my helping him). But if, in addition, we are both disposed to help helpers, and I help him, my act will enhance my individual fitness because it identifies me as a suitable person to be helped when the occasion arises. Thus genes which disposed a person to treat anyone as a brother if he acted like one could now spread independently of kin selection, because of the selective advantage of reciprocal altruism.

Kin selection is interesting because it explains how altruism could be selected for even when it is genuinely self-sacrificial: The altruism that is selected for is the kind that Bishop Butler says self love would veto and the kind that Ayn Rand would execrate. Trivers' theory, on the other hand, aims to show that altruistic acts merely appear to be self-sacrificial: Altruism benefits the altruist because it labels him for other altruists as a potential recipient of altruistic acts. His view is like the venerable claim of moral philosophers that virtue, contrary to appearances, really best serves one's self-interest. However, the "virtue" with which Trivers is concerned is greatly contracted: His reciprocal altruists are nicer to nice people and therefore run lower overall risks. Trivers' reciprocal altruists should not be expected to act from motives of rational self-interest, for the motive through which the genetic program works is much more likely to be a spontaneous desire to help, however much the act as a matter of fact is in one's long-range interest. The evolved motive probably is as other-directed in the case of reciprocal altruism as it is in the case of kin altruism.

We should remember that even to enlightened nineteenth century thinkers such as Thomas Huxley the results of natural selection and the demands of morality were at war with one another:[8] Evolution produced the beast in us, ever ready to grab and kill for the sake of personal survival, whereas ethics was a fragile thing, nurtured by intelligence and civilization, representing a higher and non-evolutionary level of development. Is it by nature that Man wants to attribute the beast in him to nature and the noble, just and kind sentiments to his own creation or discovery? Biologists now are producing theories of the origin of just those gentler and kinder sentiments which Huxley fancied transcended evolution. Huxley's conclusion reflects the ancient Christian view that Man, or at least what is worthwhile about him, is not part of nature. Behind my sympathy for sociobiological hypotheses is a conviction that Man is part of nature and that it is the task of philosophers as well as scientists to increase our understanding of how this is so.

Some recent writers believe Huxley was partly correct, that while there do exist innate dispositions toward kindness and fairness, these are insufficient to motivate the mutual restraint on self-interest that society requires of a system of social morality. The psychologist Donald Campbell took this position.[9] Campbell argues plausibly that innate selfishness is still a stronger force than innate altruism, hence that even our rational desires, if not controlled by societal inhibitions, will on balance be socially destructive. His view implies that a minimally adequate social morality requires other-regarding moral dispositions, some of which are innate (in the sense, we may suppose, defined in Section 6.3), and some of which are the product of social conditioning. As a causal hypothesis, this position seems to me correct as far as it goes. However, Campbell and the whole profession of social scientists, excepting a few sociologists, ignore group egoism, which is the most important component of innate human sociality and an essential source of prosocial motivation which, just like altruism, requires cultural reinforcement. It is characteristic of individualist, Anglo-American social scientists and biologists that altruism is the only innate norm they consider: Group loyalty is essentially a tribal, collectivist motive, altruism essentially a private transaction between individual altruist and recipient.

Evolutionary explanations of morality invite familiar kinds of mistakes. For if sociobiology sets the stage for sorting norms into those which are "from nature" and those which are "from nurture," I suppose we must look forward to a whole new crop of romantic evolutionists, armed with theories about the evolution of altruism, the free market economy, or whatever, which never were available to Herbert Spencer or John Fisk. They will say, if an early human ancestor was genetically disposed to help good guys and be ruthless to bad guys, he had increased fitness, but if he was genetically disposed to love his enemy and to turn the other cheek, he had a smaller chance of passing on his DNA. An individual's DNA, if it could choose its host, would prefer Ghengis Kahn to Christ. Accepting their DNA as their moral authority, the romantic evolutionists may opt for the morality of Ghengis Khan. Or they may say, with kin selection in mind, that it is natural to value human lives in inverse ratio to how far away they are, and therefore nothing to be ashamed of.

If someone is inclined to accept moral views whose genetic causal component (assuming he can

179

identify it) catches his fancy, and to reject those
with "mere cultural origins," we can ask what causes
him to believe that evolutionary moral principle.
One hopes these causes are more on the side of
nurture. Romantic anti-evolutionists will take the
opposite view and maintain that normative behavior
resulting from natural selection should be replaced
by a higher morality that transcends evolution. The
biological claims themselves imply neither of these
positions. The legitimate function of causal
explanations of morality, whether they be genetic or
cultural explanations, is not to yield moral conclusions but to help us understand the phenomena, i.e.,
normative behavior.

6.5 Inviting Causation. If getting and losing
moral beliefs is as I have described, we need to
revise our conception of the aims and limits of
moral argument. Confronted with moral disagreement,
we seek agreement (and accuracy) about the facts and
about our logic. Given agreement about these, if
moral disagreement persists, it now depends on
environmental and genetic causes of how much we care
about or fear certain things. What rational people
can do has been moved to a deeper level. They can
put themselves in positions to experience the
competing elements of the situation. In Chapter
Five I argued that this is not just a matter of
learning new facts from experience; it is being
influenced by the experiences themselves.

Is being influenced by relevant experiences less
rational than being influenced by relevant facts?
("Relevant" here means causally relevant given a
background of antecedent beliefs and attitudes, and
also relevant to the issue in a common sense way.)
An ideal evaluator would want to acquire his normative beliefs on the basis of the joint effect of
everything that can have an effect. Since torture
and drugs, if they would have an influence at all,
would work on each side of the issue, a rational
evaluator would spare himself a double dose of
torture. Opening oneself to causes is irrational if
it is done one-sidedly, such as spending time with
police but not with the people who accuse them of
brutality or discourtesy. Selected experiences are
like selected facts and a moral judgment can be

biased by either. To investigate a moral problem is to invite oneself to be caused to end up with a particular attitude; for factual beliefs are as much potential causes as experiences. What rationality requires is that one maximize promising inputs without making mistakes; and that the moral disposition one finds oneself acquiring is, as much as possible, the joint effect of everything causally relevant to it. There is no point in insisting on "morally relevant" instead of or in addition to "causally relevent," for if something is morally relevant but causes nothing (whatever this might mean), eo ipso it has no effect on decision. The unattainable ideal is to be an omnipercipient ideal experiencer, not just an ideal observer.

An omniscient ideal observer may know such propositions as "Police officers P, P'... said discourteous things ABC on N occasions in circumstances C, C'...," etc. F. C. Sharp suggested, however, that knowledge by description is an inferior surrogate for knowledge by acquaintance: Merely knowing propositions is a less perfect encounter with the reality one's moral judgment is about. If we understand the matter this way experience is superior to knowledge of propositions and a truly ideal observer would be omnipercipient as well as omniscient. What such an enhanced ideal observer is doing is subjecting himself to potential causes by way of both propositions and experiences. In a dispute over capital punishment two educated people may know the facts and also agree about the basic principles involved; but one of them may not appreciate the facts in the way the other does. A good part of what lies behind the importance of "appreciating the facts" is the causal superiority of experience over knowledge of propositions. Appreciation of the facts about capital punishment is much more likely to result from witnessing an execution or, on the other side, seeing a friend murdered for money, than it is from further argument.

But is not a moral belief produced in this way irrational? I have been arguing that it is not, indeed, that an ideal observer would be omnipercipient and expose himself to everything likely to alter his disposition. However, this position requires a number of qualifications, the first a consequence of the fact that we can more nearly attain omniscience than omnipercipience. The second is the requirement to apply the same canons of good reasoning and unbiasedness in the context of experiences as we do in the context of beliefs.

In cases where important normative decisions must be reached by means of a democratic process it is reasonable to restrict evidence to what is accessible to all parties to the decision. Thus in many issues of interpersonal morality where a consensus must be reached or laws must be made, rationality can require that knowledge of propositions count more than experience. This would not be so if we could "know by acquaintance" as much, as readily, and as cheaply as we can "know by description." But I cannot have everyone's experiences or even have experiences that resemble those of everyone. I cannot have the experiences of a veal calf or a deposed president. It would be counterproductive to seek the experience of being executed or starving to death in Bangladesh. Moreover, the onesidedness of our experience is less easily corrected than the onesidedness of factual belief. Finally, our lack of omnipercipience produces a certain resentment at being told such things as "you would know the fitting punishment if you had been mugged as I have been" or "you, who are white, can never understand the depths of the injustice suffered by black people." I am being told I can never be qualified. The resentment is exacerbated by the requirement, placed on us by a democratic society, of often having an equal official voice about these matters and being responsible for one's decision. So we usually say that what is equally accessible to all in books or speeches is sufficient for the rationality of moral decisions in which a number of people must take part.

A society may go so far as to say that a reliable moral (and legal) judge should be someone who has not had particularly intimate personal experience of either side of the issue, on the ground that otherwise he would be "biased." This kind of bias is really just incomplete research, it is the analogue of knowing the facts on only one side of the case and would be eliminated by the omnipercipience we know we cannot have. Factual propositions about both sides of a moral issue are public, sharable, safe, and can be got by the hundreds in an evening from books. Hence, in an environment of incomplete trust and democratic participation we limit the grounds for moral decisions to knowledge by description, not because brute experience cannot be part of the basis for a rational moral judgment but for the reasons given. I suspect that this is why many people are ambivalent about the suggestion that criminals' just punishments be set by their victims. We rightly say that ineffable experiences cannot count as reasons for public policy; but at the same time we know that if a victim could have equal access to the lifetime experiences of criminals, other victims, potential criminals and victims (and also satisfied the usual conditions of rationality and knowledge), then he could not possibly have a better basis for a judgment of proper punishment.

Given the above qualifications, I am arguing for the integration of experience and reasons. I am not suggesting that an experience is a kind of reason: Reasons are public in a way experiences are not; two persons can have equal access to one reason, or at least to the words that express it, but not to one experience. Nevertheless, the dualism of "influences" and "rational considerations," of causes versus reasons, as it is usually understood, is indefensible. On the one hand we have been taught to think of causes, influences, and conditioning as irrational, as sources of moral error and stupid attitudes toward sex, money, and politics. On the other hand we are taught that rational moral beliefs are based on "good reasons" or are the conclusions of sound moral arguments. This bifurcation is just all wrong. It is not that we shouldn't employ reasons and arguments, particularly as we acquire new knowledge. But this is just one half of a story the other half of which is equally respectable. For unless a person is made to care about the interets of other people, about the suffering of animals, or about his country, moral argument will be of no avail. The premises will not move him, or will not move him enough.

Being rational about morality is a matter of inviting the causation of moral beliefs where invitations are tendered to potential causes that are accurate (in the case of beliefs), as complete as possible, and which meet the standard criteria for evidence and clear thinking. Moral intellec- tualists who enjoy thinking of causes in terms of "brain washing" and the administration of diabolical drugs should ask themselves what they are about when they morally educate their children by example and by the "right" experiences. Leading my child (or an adult) to see and feel is not less rational than giving him a premises-to-conclusion moral argument. I am not brain washing in the one case and invoking the sweet light of reason in the other. However, straightforwardly subjecting a person to causes operates on a deeper level. Argument attempts to get him to classify executions, hitting someone, or an endangered species, as a kind he already opposes or supports. Subjecting him to example and experi- ence attempt to get him to adopt toward a kind of thing an attitude (or degree of it) he does not already have at any level of generality. Successful moral argument presupposes agreement about princi- ples and their relative weights; one function of moral education is to produce such agreement in the first place. Hence teaching our children morality by example and by selected experiences is not less worthy or less rational than giving them arguments, for in each case we are trying to make them support what we believe is right and despise what we believe is wrong.

If I believe it is good to be kind to animals and preserve species I will show my children books and television programs which are about the wonders of animal life and which deplore hunting and cruelty. I will do my best to condition them to have the attitudes toward animals I think they ought to have. When they get older this training will also employ arguments. But argument depends on their <u>caring</u> whether, e.g., whales become extinct, on their caring about preserving what is unique, on their not caring more about the economic benefits of whaling, and on their caring about animal life in general. If they care about these things, it is because earlier something or someone made them care, or, possibly, because they are naturally inclined to care; if they do not care argument will be hopeless.

The situation is not essentially different for adults. The general moral dispositions of adults are more numerous and relatively fixed and this makes them at once more amenable to arguments in which logic and new factual information make the difference; they are less amenable to experiences designed to make them care about something they did not care about before. If it is intellectually respectable to inculcate morality in children by example and experience, it is equally respectable in adults. Adults often are embarrassed to admit they have been "swayed" or influenced by experiences, e.g., by proximity to new life styles or to the daily lives and problems of police officers, prisoners, landlords or welfare recipients. They may think it a sign of irrationality or weakness to admit, "I knew what the facts were all along, but since X happened to me I have come to feel differently about the matter." It seems to me, however, that when a person always demands moral arguments and refuses to risk entering situations in which he may become "sentimental" or be "swayed," what he is doing is announcing that his moral education has ceased. He is saying that he has his principles and all reason will permit is plugging in new factual premises, turning his logical crank, and grinding out conclusions. He is resolving to be unresponsive and pigheaded in the name of rationality.

Chapter VI: NOTES

1. See Charles Taylor, THE EXPLANATION OF BEHAVIOR
    (London and Henley: Routledge and Kegan
    Paul, 1964), Chapter 2, and Norman Malcolm,
    "The Conceivability of Mechanism," PHILO-
    SOPHICAL REVIEW, 77 (1968), pp. 45-72.

2. Charles Stevenson, ETHICS AND LANGUAGE (New
    Haven: Yale University Press, 1944), Chap-
    ter IX.

3. Jane van Lawick-Goodall, IN THE SHADOW OF MAN
    (Boston: Houghton Mifflin Company, 1971),
    pp. 182-183.

4. Joseph Shepher, "Mate Selection Among Second
    Generation Kibbutz Adolescents and Adults:
    Incest Avoidance and Negative Imprinting,"
    ARCHIVES OF SEXUAL BEHAVIOR, 1 (1971), pp.
    293-307.

5. W. D. Hamilton, "The Genetical Evolution of
    Social Behavior" (I and II), JOURNAL OF
    THEORETICAL BIOLOGY, 7 (1964), pp. 1-52.

6. Hamilton, op. cit.

7. Robert L. Trivers, "The Evolution of Reciprocal
    Altruism," QUARTERLY REVIEW OF BIOLOGY, 46
    (1971), pp. 35-57.

8. Thomas H. Huxley, op. cit.

9. Donald T. Campbell, "On the Conflicts Between
    Biological and Social Evolution and Between
    Psychology and Moral Tradition," AMERICAN
    PSYCHOLOGIST, 30 (1975), pp. 1103-1126.